Early Praise for *Practical A/B Testing*

A great resource—especially for those that intuitively understand what A/B testing is but haven't had direct, firsthand experience with it.

➤ **Martin Snyder**
   VP of Engineering

A great dive into the foundational concepts to get started with A/B testing. This book includes practical examples of an important step in product development.

➤ **Sonia Namlera**
   Product Manager

This book is a helpful entry to the world of A/B testing that will help your product or engineering teams get started.

➤ **Mali Joneanse**
   Software Engineer

Practical A/B Testing

Creating Experimentation-Driven Products

Leemay Nassery

The Pragmatic Bookshelf

Raleigh, North Carolina

Many of the designations used by manufacturers and sellers to distinguish their products are claimed as trademarks. Where those designations appear in this book, and The Pragmatic Programmers, LLC was aware of a trademark claim, the designations have been printed in initial capital letters or in all capitals. The Pragmatic Starter Kit, The Pragmatic Programmer, Pragmatic Programming, Pragmatic Bookshelf, PragProg and the linking *g* device are trademarks of The Pragmatic Programmers, LLC.

Every precaution was taken in the preparation of this book. However, the publisher assumes no responsibility for errors or omissions, or for damages that may result from the use of information (including program listings) contained herein.

For our complete catalog of hands-on, practical, and Pragmatic content for software developers, please visit *https://pragprog.com*.

The team that produced this book includes:

CEO: Dave Rankin
COO: Janet Furlow
Managing Editor: Tammy Coron
Development Editor: Vanya Wryter
Copy Editor: L. Sakhi MacMillan
Layout: Gilson Graphics
Founders: Andy Hunt and Dave Thomas

For sales, volume licensing, and support, please contact *support@pragprog.com*.

For international rights, please contact *rights@pragprog.com*.

ISBN-13: 979-8-88865-008-0
Book version: P1.0—May 2023

Contents

Acknowledgments

Special thank you to everyone who helped evaluate the technical aspects of the book: Ching-Wei Chen, Martin Synder, Eskil Forsell, Sonia Namlera, and Mali Joneanse. I very much appreciate your time and thoughtful feedback. Thank you!

Thank you to my editor, Vanya Wryter, without whom the book wouldn't have been possible. Your encouragement and profound feedback taught me how to approach the writing process. I will forever remember our Japanese lasagna recipe analogy.

Finally, I want to thank my friends and family, especially my parents, who A/B tested croissants with me. Life is an aggregate of many small and big experiments, and none would be valid without you all.

Preface

What happens when you build a new feature, then make an assumption about the impact on the product? Your prediction may be right. Or your prediction may be wrong. How do you know for certain that the change had a positive influence on your product metrics?

If these questions resonate, even in the slightest bit, there's a solution: A/B testing. When you build the capability to practice A/B testing on your product, you can measure how a change influenced key product and business metrics. With this evaluation methodology, you and anyone on your team can test new ideas and measure the impact of that change with data.

Speaking of new feature ideas, I had a grand idea to evolve a product in 2019.

This idea, although not very novel since many other products had already implemented such a feature, was to build a personalized For You homepage. At the time, I was leading a small and talented engineering team responsible for the personalization features on the X1 video product at Comcast Corporation.

After a few months of kicking the idea around with engineering and product leads, we met resistance because it needed to be clarified how the For You homepage would impact critical product and business metrics. The natural next step was, of course, to build an A/B testing platform. We used A/B testing as a Trojan horse into the product. Instead of asking to launch the For You homepage, we leaned on A/B testing to provide the data and user insights needed to convince those who thought otherwise.

It was tough.

From the day the test kicked off, it took exactly one year to launch the For You homepage to all users. Why did it take so long? First, we leveraged A/B testing in an organization that historically did not use this methodology to evaluate product ideas. In some product organizations, enabling A/B testing may be more of a cultural challenge than an engineering challenge. Motivating teams to change their habits and trust the A/B testing platform can be challenging, especially if they were accustomed to simply launching their changes straight to production for all their users to engage with immediately.

When you build a product, you want to delight your users with seamless and easy-to-use experiences. How do you know which changes are improving the user experience? How do you know you're not degrading the experience? Or, how do you know the product is optimal for all demographics and not simply geared toward the majority? These are questions that A/B testing can answer.

This book will provide a practical approach to implementing A/B testing so that you can understand the impact of your changes on your user, product, and business metrics.

How to Get Started

The only thing worse than not A/B testing is waiting years to build the perfect engineering platform. You can actually get started with very little. You just need the fundamentals.

This book will introduce you to the core concepts—the anatomy of an A/B test, audience segmentation logic, and the infrastructure to serve and monitor performance. You'll learn how to define a hypothesis, create eligibility criteria, and select metrics to demonstrate the impact of the test.

Understanding the practical examples detailed in this book will help you integrate this experimentation methodology into your product. You'll be able to go into conversations with your engineering and product teams with the right vocabulary and tactics to get started.

What to Expect

This book will not teach you everything there is to know, but it will help you get more comfortable with the key components and concepts so you can kickstart your A/B testing journey. Whether you're an engineer, manager, or product owner, this book is a starting point, overflowing with techniques and practical ways for you to approach the A/B testing process.

Specifically, we'll cover these topics in the following chapters:

- Chapter 1: the rationale for running A/B tests.

- Chapter 2: the basic anatomy of an A/B test.

- Chapter 3: the various types of A/B tests.

- Chapter 4: the data requirements for running A/B tests and visualizing test results.

- Chapter 5: the factors to consider when building an A/B testing platform in-house versus a third-party solution.

- Chapter 6: the tactics to cultivate a test-friendly culture.

To illustrate these concepts, you'll find references to a fictitious company called CableMax. The CableMax narrative is highly influenced by the experiences I already alluded to—my time at Comcast. The majority of the examples throughout this book are anchored on this experience of building an in-house solution to run experiments on a video product used by millions. When you're ready to get started, you'll have the perfect blueprint.

It's worth noting that the CableMax use case will also provide a means for you to practice what you've learned by reading the sidebars for relevant tasks throughout this book, so don't forget to check those out!

OK, So What's Next?

If you're not currently A/B testing, this book will help identify some of the tools and techniques you need to move forward. By learning from the practical examples and exploring how they may apply to your product, you'll be A/B testing changes sooner than you think.

Let's get started!

CHAPTER 1

Why You Should A/B Test

A/B testing is a key part of product development. On the surface, it may seem like a complex methodology that requires fancy tools and elaborate engineering systems. However, this isn't the case if you're just getting started. You don't need to know every detail of A/B testing to integrate this practice into your product development process, but understanding the fundamentals is necessary.

This book will expose you to concepts that can help kickstart incorporating A/B testing into your product. We'll lay out the anatomy of a test and the core components required to facilitate A/B testing. We'll explore practical concepts and strategies to incorporate A/B testing within your organization, starting with the many advantages of this experimentation methodology. Specifically, this chapter includes the following:

- How your team can benefit from A/B testing.

- How you can gain user insights you didn't even think to seek at the start of a project.

- How you can use A/B testing to catch engineering system vulnerabilities earlier rather than later.

- How you can leverage A/B testing as a risk management tool.

To further illustrate the advantages of A/B testing, you'll have the role of analyst for the personalization team at CableMax. Although CableMax is a fictitious company, it's loosely based on a real-life context that used A/B testing to improve the experience for a user-facing product. There will be analyst tasks related to your role at CableMax to get some hands-on experience.

So, without further ado, let's get started!

What Is A/B Testing?

A/B testing is an online controlled experiment that measures the impact of a change on a subset of users. An effective A/B test is one where you feel confident in making decisions based on the results.

An A/B test, also referred to as an experiment, in its simplest form consists of two groups of users, as shown in the following image. The first group is the control variant which includes users who receive the unchanged functionality or product experience. The second group consists of users who receive a new feature or change that is up for evaluation, known as the test variant. Both the test and control variants need to be randomized to ensure that the users assigned to each group are similar statistically, allowing for higher confidence when measuring the effect of the experiment. If the variants are not properly randomized, then you wouldn't know with high certainty that the changes evaluated in the experiment caused an increase or decrease in key metrics.

User Population

User population excluding the control and test variants; these users receive the same product experience as the control.

Control variant users are randomly sampled and receive an unchanged product experience.

Test variant users are randomly sampled and receive an alternative experience that is up for evaluation.

Now to determine the effectiveness of the change, you'll use metrics to compare the engagement of the test variant to the control variant. Your metrics and variants are closely tied together. Without proper variant randomization, your test results may represent an inaccurate estimate of the effect of the change, as they could be biased toward a specific user population or other unknown factors. We'll be looking more closely at A/B testing terminology in *Learn the Fundamentals of an A/B Test*, but for now, let's start with a basic understanding.

You're evaluating changes on real users and measuring the outcome using data. The change that is evaluated as part of the experiment could include:

- A new UX design to a user-facing product.
- A new feature or change to an existing feature.

- A new software architecture that, for example, improves the efficiency of the engineering system under the hood but, ideally, should be transparent to the user.

If you're building user-facing products, your goal is to improve the user experience and create business impact. When you leverage A/B testing to evaluate a change, the test results allow you to measure if you're meeting your intended goals.

Who Should Run A/B Tests

Everyone and anyone should run A/B tests: product owners, engineers, engineering managers, designers, data scientists, user researchers, and really, anyone who has the desire to learn about the product they're building. If you have a theory and the desire to prove your theory is true, then you should utilize A/B testing.

When you should run an A/B test is subjective. You may prefer all user-facing changes, whether big or small, to be A/B tested. Or you may choose a less conservative approach: A/B test more significant changes. For more minor changes, compare your metrics before versus after the change was rolled out to all your users. It really just depends on your use case and what type of questions you're looking to answer.

Here are a few points to consider when deciding on whether to evaluate a change with an A/B test:

- If your product is new or you're testing a brand-new domain, your metrics may be more volatile. In this case, it's better to start measuring changes early as you iterate on the product over time.

- If your product is mature, your metrics may not be as sensitive to changes, making it a bit harder to move the needle. That's not to say that you shouldn't leverage A/B testing. You may want to opt for an equivalence test, which will be discussed in detail in *Select the Right Type of Experiment*.

- If you're keen on protecting the user from an unintentional degradation in the product experience, use A/B testing to gather data insights into the performance of change on a subset of users first.

- If you find it necessary to introduce the change at a lower scale first, to evaluate the risk or the potential for uncovering scale issues before it's available for all your users.

If you're still wondering whether you should evaluate a change using the A/B testing methodology, consider the following questions that data from an A/B test could answer:

- How did this change impact key business metrics?
- How are specific minority user groups affected by the new feature?
- How did this change influence engagement on other surfaces of the product?

This is all to say, if you have questions about the usage and the impact of changes made to the product, then you're the perfect candidate to run an A/B test.

Beginning Your Analyst Role

You were recently hired at CableMax, a company with a large footprint in the United States, providing video services to millions of users.

Given the company's size, you'd assume there would be a sophisticated A/B testing platform that supports the innovation made to the video product. That's not the case. Even big companies need help getting started with A/B testing.

The engineering and product teams at CableMax want to better understand how new features influence user engagement and impact key business metrics. This is why they've asked you to help them push their A/B testing practices forward. You'll start with a team known to push changes straight to production, with little evaluation or measurement beforehand: the personalization team.

The personalization team is responsible for features that enable users to quickly access content to watch on the company's flagship video product. To get an idea of the user experience you're providing analyst support for, see the image on page 5. The colored squares represent individual TV shows or movies that are personalized based a user's taste and watch history.

Since you're a new hire, let's set the stage a bit more.

It's clear what is missing from the video product: a personalized For You homepage. CableMax users expect good value for what they pay for, so naturally, you want to make it as easy as possible to engage with. The For You homepage will be a single location where the user can find recommended content just for them, instead of the typical editorial experience that is "one-size-fits-all."

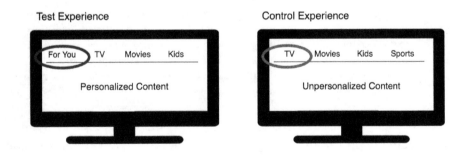

This is a great idea, but all ideas, whether great or not-so-great, should be A/B tested. And that's exactly what the team at CableMax decides to do: launch a For You A/B test on the video product.

To evaluate the For You homepage, users in the test variant will receive the For You experience (left). Users in the control variant will receive the unchanged, unpersonalized experience (right). See the following image.

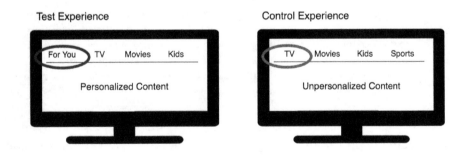

Now, before you dive further into the For You A/B test, check out your first task as an analyst on the personalization team by taking a look at *Analyst Task: How to Prepare for an A/B Test*, shown on page 6.

Now that you're starting to think like an analyst for the For You experiment, let's explore why A/B testing benefits you, your team, and your users.

Evaluating Your Ideas

When you want to persuade someone to do something, it's best to start with why that "something" is useful. And that's precisely the goal in this first

Analyst Task: How to Prepare for an A/B Test

You see personalization everywhere—Netflix, Spotify, Pinterest, Etsy, and Peloton. Name the brand, and you'll without a doubt find some degree of a personalized homepage on the product. Although this is the case, it's best to be prepared. You never know, maybe the For You implementation won't serve the needs of CableMax users. How will you, as the analyst for the personalization team, ensure that the For You A/B test will be successful? Success in this context means you've learned as much as possible about the impact of a change to your users and metrics.

When preparing for an A/B test, make sure you do the following to ensure success:

- Partner closely with the user research team as they may have already conducted studies that complement or validate the idea that's being evaluated. UX researchers are trained in collecting insights from qualitative studies and analyzing data to help inform product decisions. Make these humans your best friends, as their studies could be inspiration for future A/B tests.

- Ask your fellow data engineers if important data sets are available to query for ad hoc analysis. Nothing's worse than realizing you need to gather deeper insights beyond your metrics and lack the data to do so.

- Align on expectations for launching the feature with the team and key stakeholders. What happens if the test results are neutral, meaning there wasn't a substantial negative or positive increase in the key success metrics? Would the feature launch be gated on substantial positive gains?

- Ask your engineering team if there's any infrastructure or system that's at risk as a result of evaluating this new feature in production on a subset of users. Do you have monitoring in place to keep an eye on the systems that the For You homepage is dependent on? If there is cause for concern, it may impact your test results, so it's better to know the vulnerabilities sooner rather than later.

chapter: focusing on the *why*. Why the notion of A/B testing changes made to your product is beneficial and something you should invest in and spend time on.

Maybe you're the cautious type: triple checking you haven't forgotten your keys, always creating a pro/con list before making any decisions, and avoiding risk at all costs. If this is the case, consider A/B testing a tool to vet your ideas, reducing the risk of launching a feature that could degrade the experience for your users (or engineering systems). Let A/B testing be your safety net.

On the flip side, let's say you and risk are two peas in a pod. You like to be bold and launch any idea that comes to mind. You feel fulfilled knowing you're making changes to the product that others would never have the courage to.

If this resonates with you, A/B testing will enable you to dream big and evaluate your grand ideas on a subset of users.

Let's see how A/B testing exposes the ability to validate ideas from multiple stakeholders.

Assessing Multiple Designs at Once

Sometimes you may find yourself in a situation with far too many cooks in the kitchen. These cooks usually have lots of opinions. A feeling or experience typically backs these opinions. However, it's not enough to have a feeling. It's not enough to assume an idea is the best way to evolve a product, especially when there are multiple versions or designs in mind. Instead of picking one based on a feeling, use A/B testing to assess multiple versions or ideas.

When configuring a test to have multiple variants, also referred to as versions, that are all up for evaluation, be mindful of how many changes you're incorporating within one variant.

To illustrate, see the following image. Notice variants A, B, and C all have one variable that has changed compared to the control experience: the buy button's location. Maybe your peer product manager strongly feels that the buy button should be located in the top right of the mobile app or your teammate would prefer to position the buy button in the middle. If a metric increased for variant B, you could assume that the change resulted from the buy button moving to the center of the page. Variants A, B, and C are good examples of evaluating multiple approaches simultaneously.

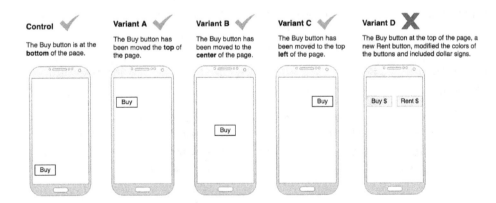

Now take note of the changes in variant D:

- The buy button has moved to the top of the page.
- The buy button color differs from A, B, and C.

- The rent button was added to the right of the buy button.
- The dollar sign symbol is an addition that doesn't exist in the other three variants.

With these four changes, how will you know which aspect of variant D caused a shift in the metrics compared to variants A, B, and C? Was it the introduction of the rent button? Or was it all of the changes in aggregate that influenced your metrics? Maybe if the dollar sign were included in variants A, B, or C, they would outperform D.

This example illustrates that the composition of your test variants matters, especially if you want to pinpoint which change influenced your metrics.

Let's explore the next benefit of A/B testing: learning about your users and how they engage with the product.

Gaining User Insights

A/B testing won't solve all your problems. It will, however, solve a few of them.

With A/B testing, you lower your risk of launching changes that could degrade the user experience. You'll also gain user insights you had no idea you needed. It won't replace the need for a product vision, but it will help inform whether your strategy and roadmap meet the needs of your users and your business.

When you have an idea of how you'd like to evolve a product, you typically believe it will improve the experience for all your users. Sometimes your intuition is correct, and sometimes it's wrong. How do you know your idea is improving the experience for all your users if you don't measure the outcome?

Returning to the For You A/B Test

Let's return to the For You A/B Test to explore how the new feature influenced user engagement on the video product.

It's challenging to navigate to a user's recently watched TV shows in the current video product experience. Although many products have a personalized homepage that solves this problem, it's not always guaranteed the implementation will improve the user experience. This is why you're A/B testing the For You homepage. Your goal is to gather user insights into how the For You homepage impacted both the user experience and key business metrics. Let's look at *Analyst Task: What are Your Early Predictions?* on page 9.

Analyst Task: What are Your Early Predictions?

Before the For You A/B test results are revealed, what is your prediction?

Knowing what you know this far into your journey as an analyst at CableMax, do you think the test variant will outperform the control experience? Would you expect the test results to suggest that all the users in the test variant have a notable increase in consumption of TV shows and movies when compared to the users in the control variant? Or do you think there will be a neutral or negative impact of introducing a For You homepage to the video product?

Discovering Surprising User Insights

Let's see if your initial prediction was accurate.

The summary of the initial findings from the A/B test is underwhelming. There was a slight increase in content consumption, also referred to as video plays, for users that received the For You homepage.

More precisely, the slight increase was in the 1 to 2 percent range. Underwhelmed doesn't even begin to express the sentiment of the personalization team. The team expected mammoth-sized increases in consumption when comparing the test variant to the control variant, not just a slight increase.

The initial results for the For You A/B test, shown in the following image, compares the content consumption of the control variant to the test variant.

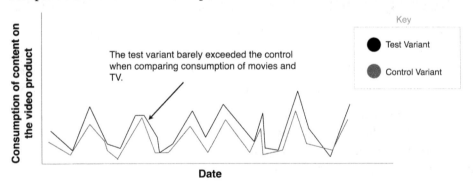

Before these initial results, the team felt liberated and pleased with making it this far. They never considered that introducing the For You homepage would only result in minimal improvements.

Of course, you could say a slight increase is better than no increase. However, it still doesn't feel *right*. The editorial experience is drastically different from the personalized homepage—so drastic that you would expect metrics to differ at a higher degree.

Comparing Predictions

Were you surprised by the insights from the initial test results? Did you predict that introducing a personalized homepage would increase consumption for all users—taking note of the word "all" users? When compared to an editorial experience, why wouldn't a personalized experience increase consumption for everyone?

Did you consider the chance for a decrease in consumption compared to the control group? Anything is possible. Sometimes the effect of the changes measured in an A/B test differs from what you originally predicted. Regardless if your prediction is right or wrong, the goal is to gain more insights about your product.

Or did you predict exactly what was observed in the test results: a slight increase in video plays for the users in the test variant? If this is the case, maybe your reasoning for this prediction was that a personalized For You homepage wasn't something the users needed. Perhaps the control experience met the user's content discovery needs.

Now that we have this initial data, we'll dive into further analysis to understand better why the For You A/B test results were lower than expected.

Conducting Additional Analysis for Deeper User Insights

Performing additional analysis for an A/B test is common, especially when introducing bigger changes to a product. The results of an A/B test tell you what happened, but they don't typically tell you why it happened. To understand why, you may need to do subsequent analysis.

In *Interface with Data and Visualizing Results*, we'll detail best practices for interfacing with data so that it's easy to conduct additional data analysis; until then, let's explore how analyzing subgroups within the test variants enabled us to understand why the initial For You test results were so low.

Assessing the For You Homepage on High Consumption Users

The For You homepage is a significant change to CableMax's flagship video product. Introducing this new experience changes how users navigate and discover the content they want to watch on TV. With such a significant change, you're wondering how it had such little impact on the test metrics.

As the analyst on the personalization team, you've decided to dive deeper into the data.

Your first step will be to split the users within the test and control variants based on how much content they consume on the video product. See the following image. This split will create subgroups from the original test and control variants that will be referred to as "high consumption users" versus "low consumption users."

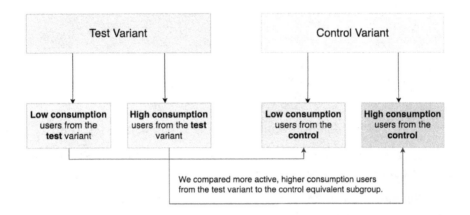

Once these subgroups are created, you'll compute each subgroup's total videos watched metric. You'll also be ready for your next analyst task, *Analyst Task: What Will You Learn from These Subgroups?*, in the sidebar.

Analyst Task: What Will You Learn from These Subgroups?

What do you predict you'll learn from splitting the users into subgroups? Do you think there will be different consumption patterns with users in the higher-consumption user groups when compared to the control and test variants?

Think about this before the answer is revealed.

When analyzing the high consumption users subgroup for both the test and control, the test variant had notably higher consumption compared to similar users in the control group who also watched a lot of content but did not receive the personalized For You homepage. And for users in the test variant who watched minimal content, their consumption was very similar to the equivalent subgroup in the control variant. See the graph shown on page 12.

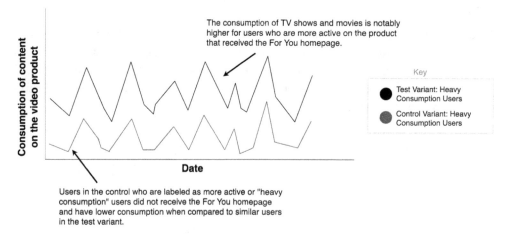

For You A/B Test: Heavy Consumption Subgroup Analysis

The consumption of TV shows and movies is notably higher for users who are more active on the product that received the For You homepage.

Key

● Test Variant: Heavy Consumption Users

● Control Variant: Heavy Consumption Users

Consumption of content on the video product

Date

Users in the control who are labeled as more active or "heavy consumption" users did not receive the For You homepage and have lower consumption when compared to similar users in the test variant.

To summarize, with this additional user insight you've learned that:

- The For You homepage performs substantially well for users who watched a lot of content on the video product.

- The For You homepage does not perform as well for users who do not watch as much content.

Think for a moment about what the graph represents.

The users who watch a lot of content watch even more content when provided with the For You homepage. The consumption habits of users who watch minimal content on the video product were unaffected when presented with the For You homepage. This is an interesting user insight!

A/B testing is a force multiplier. The more you learn about your users and how they interact with the product, the more informed you'll be about future innovations. For example, maybe you'll decide to invest time in the cohort of minimally active users on the video product. Your goal would be to shift their consumption so they're more engaged, watching more TV shows and movies. In its current state, the For You homepage may not influence this specific user group; therefore, time should be spent on alternative strategies to achieve the desired outcome. You could suggest that your team implement a new algorithm, or modifications could be made to a different area of the product to increase users' consumption habits.

The Dangers of Averages

On a separate but related point, here's a quick tangent on the unforeseen dangers of computing averages.

When you average the data to compute a metric, consider outliers, especially in systems that may have unknown or unpredictable behavior. If the data includes outliers, it distorts the metrics when averaging all data points together.

Computing averages may also hide user behavior, especially in the early stages of practicing A/B testing on your product. If this is the case, always double-check your test results.

In an article written by data scientist Eric Luellen, titled "Why Averages Are Often Wrong," he states:

Averages are misleading when used to compare different groups, apply group behavior to an individual scenario, or when there are numerous outliers in the data. The root causes of these problems appear to be over-simplification and rationalizations—what people want to believe. We know from statistics, and it's more modern sibling machine learning, that outcomes are based on causal associations, that those causal associations are complex by being multiple and dynamic, and they are far easier to measure historically than predictively.[1]

Hindsight is everything, and for the For You A/B test, you might have assumed that all users would benefit from this feature. In reality, the users who used the product less were driving the test results to be somewhat unremarkable at first sight.

Building More Inclusive Products

You can learn so much about your users and how they engage with your product by evaluating changes in the scope of an A/B test. You can discover behavior patterns of specific user groups at a much larger scale than a user research study would provide. This lets you better serve the needs of your users—all of your users.

Now, what does it mean to create an inclusive product? It means you're building a product that caters to a wide range of diverse users. Ideally, your product, whatever it may be, is in the hands of all people, not just a particular demographic.

The truth is, it's inevitable that exclusion lurks in the shadows, in the unseen crevices or hidden nooks of an engineering system. Even if you think you've

---

1. https://towardsdatascience.com/why-averages-are-often-wrong-1ff08e409a5b

built a product that is easy to use and loved by all, you are likely and unknowingly excluding a particular cohort of users. How does this look in practice? The answer is tricky because it depends on your team and product engineering practices. If you're unsure, ask yourself the following questions:

- Do you lack representation from marginalized groups within the team actually building the product?

- Do you ensure a wide range of demographics are included in your user research studies?

- Do you validate your A/B testing platforms segmentation logic for unintended imbalances of users within the test and control variants?

- Do you monitor data skew in the data sets that are training or influencing predictions produced by machine learning models?

You might be worried if you answered no to one or more of the above questions. Building an inclusive product is no easy feat. The good news is that A/B testing can help you! A/B testing can validate that your changes are optimal for all users, including the underrepresented communities.

Recognizing the Power Held by Decision Makers

Let's first recognize the power that is held by those making product decisions. When you build products that are in the hands of users, you're influencing how users interact with the product. Usually, the people harmfully impacted by a product design do not have input when the design is created.

To illustrate, consider how often you use your mobile device. Probably daily or even hourly. Now consider the size of women's hands, which are generally smaller in comparison to men's. In her TED Talk, "Why Do We Still Find Women's Voices So Scary?," Caroline Criado-Perez examines how the underrepresentation of women in tech impacts popular products. Continuing with the mobile device example, she states, "Most of the people who've been designing the phones are men, so they've been designing for the male hand size."[2]

Even if you have the best intentions while developing a product, you never know what data or circumstances you may have unintentionally missed. You could be designing a product that leaves your users vulnerable and open to harm without realizing it. That's a risk you take if you're not prioritizing building an inclusive product.

---

2. https://www.youtube.com/watch?v=AtMhtNOGNWE

Now to mitigate this risk, you have a couple of options. One tactic is to pay closer attention to the representation of employees on your team. Representation in the team building the actual product extends the decision-making table to various experiences, backgrounds, and perspectives. Another tactic is to leverage A/B testing. Let's explore this further in the next section.

Selecting User Attributes to Combat Bias

What does "using A/B testing to build inclusive products" mean in practice? The first step is to identify a category that's important to monitor and derive insights from when evaluating a change on a product. The second step is to select attributes, also referred to as dimensions, within that category.

Users engage and interact with a product differently depending on their needs, experiences, and habits. Segmenting users even into the most basic dimensions can be helpful in understanding the impact of your change, whether positive or negative. Consider the three high-level categories represented in the following image. Attributes can be derived from these higher-level categories to create user cohorts.

Once you've selected a category, choose an attribute within that category. What insight about your users and your product are you interested in learning? For instance, age or ethnicity are user attributes that could influence product engagement. If you select an attribute from the product category, such as enabling or disabling data sharing, you could answer the following questions:

- How does product engagement compare between users that have data sharing enabled versus disabled?

- How does a new feature perform for users who have data sharing disabled?

Deciding which attribute is most relevant requires reflecting on your users' needs and how a change to the product could impact those needs.

See the following table for more examples.

Attribute	Examples	Category
Socioeconomic Factors	Income, Education Level	User
Country	US, GE, UK, MX, CA	User
Gender Identity	Male, Female, Nonbinary, Transgender	User
Disability	Learning Disabilities, Hard of Hearing, Visual Impairments	User
Subscription Tenure	New User, 1 year, 2–4 years	Product
Subscription Tier	Free, Paid	Product
Device Type	iOS, Android, Web, TV, Desktop application	Product
Content Category	News, Sports, Animals, Movies, Music	Content
Consumption Volume	High, Low	Content

Table 1—Attributes to Create User Subgroups

Let's illustrate combating bias to build more inclusive products with a couple of examples from the table.

For the first example, CableMax has decided to redesign its mobile app that lets users browse TV shows and movies before purchasing a video product subscription. The change made to the experience is simple: replace text with images for a better visual representation of the content. Of course, you want to understand the impact of this change, so you suggest setting up an A/B test to evaluate the redesign. See the following image.

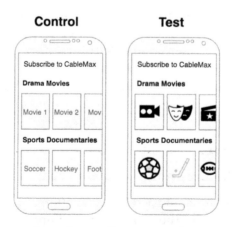

What's your first impression when reflecting on the test variant composition? How do you think adding images will affect users with lower bandwidth?

Adding images could certainly slow the app's load time, especially for those with slower internet speeds. Or did you consider the accessibility angle to this change? In this case, adding alt text to describe the image will increase accessibility for people with visual impairments or who opt for blind screen readers. Incorporating users with these dimensions would enable you to demonstrate how this change impacted specific user groups and ensure CableMax is building an inclusive product.

Let's lean into this example a bit more but from a different angle.

While redesigning the mobile app, the personalization team at CableMax decides to collect more data about the user from their interactions on the app. This change directly influences the quality of the recommendations and personalized content presented to the user as the data feeds into their machine learning algorithms. How do you think this change will impact different user groups?

Before you answer, consider a study by Lena Reinfelder, Zinaida Benenson, and Freya Gassmann detailed in the paper titled "Android and iOS users' differences concerning security and privacy" that examines varying privacy habits depending on the mobile device type.[3] The research suggests Android users are more conservative with their privacy settings than iPhone users. With this in mind, do you think this data collection change could negatively impact a particular user subgroup? Suppose Android users prefer to opt out of sharing their data. In that case, Android users are likely to have less than optimal recommendations, which could decrease a critical business or product metric. This is an excellent example of how a change that isn't necessarily cosmetic to a product's user interface could indirectly impact a metric and should be evaluated in the scope of an A/B test.

Next, we'll explore an example of incorporating specific user groups important to the business in the For You A/B test at CableMax.

Addressing the Needs of the Business

Most companies exist to make a profit. CableMax is no exception to this. As an analyst, you're very close to the business team. The data they seek insights from is the same data you seek insights from. As a rule, you've decided to bring the business stakeholders along for the ride. With each decision your team makes, you've communicated updates to them directly. No surprises.

You prepared by preemptively incorporating representation from various user dimensions in the test and control variants, specifically, dimensions that were

---

3.   https://dl.acm.org/doi/10.1145/2468356.2468502

important to the business. By doing this, you can answer questions the business stakeholders may have regarding the impact of the For You homepage on specific user groups. See the following image for examples.

Customer Age Demographics

Age Range	Control Variant	Test Variant
Age 18-25	5%	5%
Age 26-35	19%	19%
Age 36-45	23%	23%
Age 46-55	24%	23%
Age 55+	29%	30%

Customer Subscription Tier

Subscription Tier	Control Variant	Test Variant
Free	34%	32%
Premium	53%	53%
Deluxe+	10%	11%
Student	3%	4%

Customer Tenure on the Product

Product Tenure	Control Variant	Test Variant
0-5 months	13%	13%
6-11 months	9%	9%
12-23 months	12%	13%
24-35 months	10%	10%
36-47 months	7%	7%
48+ months	48%	48%

Customer Primary Language

Primary Language	Control Variant	Test Variant
English	60%	61%
Spanish	21%	18%
French	9%	9%
German	10%	11%

Questions you can answer by analyzing the engagement of these user subgroups include:

- How will consumption habits differ for users with a premium versus free subscription?

- How are new users versus tenured users impacted by the For You homepage?

- How will the For You homepage influence consumption for users in the 26–35 versus 55+ age bracket?

Now that we have predefined user subgroups, let's explore the primary language attribute to better understand consumption for users whose primary language is Spanish versus English.

Evaluating the For You A/B Test by Primary Language Subgroups

CableMax wants to increase its reach to become an international product used by millions across the globe. To achieve this goal, the video product needs to serve the needs of a wide range of users. The top two languages spoken in CableMax households are English and Spanish.

How do you think video consumption differs for users whose primary language is English versus Spanish? See the following graph.

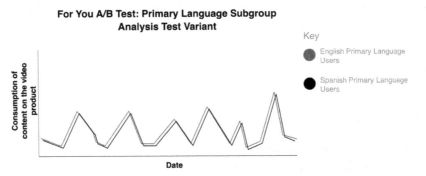

According to the graph, users from both subgroups have close similarities in consumption habits. It would be concerning if this weren't the case and the data suggested a degradation for the Spanish subgroup who received the For You homepage. The goal with this example is to trust but verify that the features you are building for your users serve the needs of not just the majority user group but also subgroups that are less prominent.

Let's weigh in with your insights as an analyst and take a look at your next task in the sidebar *Analyst Task: What Additional Attributes Should Be Considered?*

Analyst Task: What Additional Attributes Should Be Considered?

Partitioning users based on the volume of content they consumed was pivotal in understanding the impact for specific user groups. Given the attributes detailed on page 18, what other attributes about a user do you think the team should seek in addition to speaking English or Spanish? What type of questions could you answer? Remember, the goal is to demonstrate how the For You homepage performed for specific user groups.

Brainstorm a few ideas before proceeding to the next section.

For the attributes you brainstormed in the prior task, did you consider grouping users that have a habit of watching only free movies versus renting movies? If so, you would be using a user's watch history data to create the subgroups.

Another idea you may have thought of was to define subgroups based on the genre metadata associated with the content that the user most frequently watched. For example, examining whether users who preferred sports content found what they wanted to watch on the For You homepage or whether they navigated to their content via search.

Alternatively, you may have chosen user attributes such as the user's location. This type of user segmentation would enable an analysis of how the For You homepage performed in specific regions or countries.

Regardless of which attributes you choose, ensure that randomization is applied to the users allocated to each variant so that the causal effects can be determined with high probability.

Taking Risks, Being Bold

In life (and in software development), you have to be able to accept a certain amount of risk. There's the risk you'll make a self-deprecating joke to yourself while forgetting to click the mute button on a Zoom meeting. There's the risk your team will make a simple configuration change to a web service that causes a major outage. And then there's the risk that you'll launch a feature that degrades key business metrics, such as revenue or retention. You could knock on wood, cross your fingers, and hope these scenarios never happen, or you could take steps to minimize the risk. This is exactly where A/B testing can help.

A/B testing is a risk management tool. It's your best way to identify features that potentially harm your business or product metrics before the feature is available to all users.

Evaluating Your Grand Ideas, Responsibly

Maybe you're in a situation where it's hard to make big changes to the product for fear of degrading the user experience. If so, let A/B testing help you to be bold and take risks responsibly. You can use A/B testing to evaluate radical ideas. When you swing for the fences, you gain more insights into user behavior within the product.

Your team can make big bets—drastically change how users navigate and interact on the product but with the safety net of evaluating the change on a smaller user base. Instead of launching a feature to all users, launch the feature to a subset and compare their engagement to a control group of users who have the unchanged product experience. If you notice minimum or negative gains in your metrics, then don't move forward with the launch. On the other hand, if the results suggest positive gains, then you should indeed launch the feature to all users and leverage these user insights for future innovations.

When evaluating your grand ideas, consider sharing what's at risk. When you're open with the risk that you're undertaking and emphasize that the risk is reduced by evaluating the change with an A/B test, you're more likely to gain supporters.

Catch Failures, Earlier

What concerns do you have when releasing a change to production? Maybe you're worried that your engineering infrastructure can't handle the new load on the system. Or perhaps you have concerns about how the change affects specific user groups. A/B testing can help alleviate these concerns by catching failures earlier in the following areas:

- Scale: infrastructure or engineering systems could fail when changes are introduced into production.

- Accessibility: introducing a change that could degrade for users that depend on accessibility features such as captions, text enlargers, screen readers, and so on.

- Robustness: something could fail when given inputs that were unexpected when the feature or logic was initially developed (this is especially likely in a high-traffic production environment).

- Inclusion: failing to consider the needs of all the people that use the product, including minority user groups who may not be reflected in focus groups or even those that are in the room making the decisions.

Engineering systems are complex. All the variables that keep systems running when pushing code to production are sometimes forgotten or unmonitored. To illustrate this, let's circle back, once again, to the For You A/B test.

Allocating More Users to the For You A/B Test

One fine Wednesday morning, the powers that be at CableMax give you the thumbs up to allocate an additional one million users to the control and test variants. This change will increase requests for the personalization web service that serves the recommendations presented on the For You homepage.

The engineers on the team have one primary concern: can the personalization web service properly handle the additional load? To alleviate these concerns, they monitor graphs looking for abnormalities in response times and error counts.

At 5 p.m., you close your laptop, feeling a sense of pride. Increasing the A/B test to include one million additional users is a significant milestone! The more users exposed to the For You homepage, the more data you'll have and the more insights you'll gain.

Fast forward to 8 p.m., also known as "primetime" in the TV industry. The typical user gets home at around 6 p.m., cooks dinner, and then lounges on the couch at 8 p.m. to tune into their favorite TV show. During primetime, traffic to the personalization web service increases exponentially as more users turn on their TV.

But before we find out what happens next, let's take a brief pause. What do you predict will happen as a result of the increased traffic? Check out your next task in the sidebar *Analyst Task: Will Systems Survive Primetime Traffic?*

Analyst Task: Will Systems Survive Primetime Traffic?

Prior to adding the one million users, the For You page was available for about 100K users. This certainly was a big jump. What do you think will happen during primetime with the additional users added to the test?

You'll soon find out, in the upcoming section, if the infrastructure and engineering platform manages to scale.

Since this section is about catching failures early, you can predict what's to come.

The personalization web service couldn't handle the uptick in requests. See the following image. From the user's point of view, the impact was not ideal. Users received a big black screen in place of the For You homepage. Because there was a clear degradation in the user experience, the team quickly deallocated the one million users from the test.

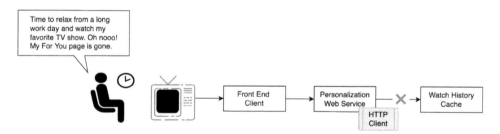

The cause for this incident was simple. The HTTP client internal to the personalization web service had the default connection pool configuration. When the HTTP client was invoked to fetch watch history data, it failed to allocate enough connections to serve the extra traffic.

Although the experiment updates were rolled back, you did learn something. You managed to avoid a major production incident by testing the engineering system's performance on a subset of users. The blast radius, or the number of impacted users, would have been far larger if you bypassed A/B testing and deployed the feature straight to production. With A/B testing, you sometimes learn what you didn't know you could learn.

How This Outcome Compares to Your Prediction

Did you think the engineering platform would survive primetime traffic? Maybe your gut reaction was *no* because increasing the number of users allocated to the test and control variants from 100K to one million is way too big of a jump. The team gained a valuable lesson: roll out changes in smaller increments—for instance, by increasing the variants by doubling the size until you've reached your goal: 200K, 400K, 800K, and so on.

Maybe you were wondering why this wasn't caught when load-testing the personalization web service before the team even started the A/B test. Well, that step was skipped. The personalization engineering team is small. You're moving fast, pushing changes to production daily, increasing the reach of personalization on the video product with each deployment to production. Load-testing and calculating the capacity the personalization web service could scale to wasn't a priority. If issues arose, you could quickly roll back, which is exactly what the team did with this primetime incident. Knowing quick rollbacks were feasible allowed your team to take this risk of launching to more users without vetting the system end-to-end.

Because the system scale issue was caught during an A/B test, a larger incident that could have impacted far more users was dodged. A/B testing (not intentionally) pressure-tested the infrastructure, and engineering systems could handle the load to support the new feature.

With A/B testing, you can prevent major decisions from becoming major mistakes.

Dispelling the Failed Experiment Myth

Humans are foundationally allergic to accepting that something didn't succeed or play out as expected. With A/B testing, this notion becomes less of a foreign concept. "Failed" experiments provide value. They give insights into how users interact with changes to a product. You can then use those lessons to pivot or change course.

Imagine the impact this mantra of "no such thing as a failed experiment" could have on teams that have a fear of action or are risk averse. A/B testing normalizes the notion of being wrong. Even a "wrong" hypothesis can lead to interesting or new insights.

The "How We Determine Product Success" post on the Netflix Technology Blog says it best. John Ciancutti, former VP of Product Engineering, states:

Sometimes our hypothesis is sound, we have a winner for our members, and we add the scale and polish necessary to get our improvement out for everyone. Or, as I mentioned, maybe the idea failed. The wonderful truth is, both outcomes help our product intuition, and therefore increase the chances that our next hypothesis will knock it out of the park.[4]

If you or your team is eager to improve the product, failure backed with results from an A/B test is the best step toward building a better product for your users.

Empowering Your Team

In a culture that embraces A/B testing, everyone can have a seat at the decision-making table. No longer are decisions made by how loud you pitch your idea in a meeting, your rank within an organization, or your connections in the political sphere of a corporate organization. Instead, anyone's ideas can be vetted through the experimentation platform, where the results inform the team how to proceed.

In a blog post by technologist and author Greg Linden, he describes a feature that was A/B tested at Amazon in the early 2000s. He perfectly articulates how A/B testing can empower your team:

Creativity must flow from everywhere. Whether you are a summer intern or the CTO, any good idea must be able to seek an objective test, preferably a test that exposes the idea to real customers.

Everyone must be able to experiment, learn, and iterate. Position, obedience, and tradition should hold no power. For innovation to flourish, measurement must rule.[5]

---

4.   https://netflixtechblog.com/how-we-determine-product-success-980f81f0047e
5.   http://glinden.blogspot.com/2006/04/early-amazon-shopping-cart.html

Let's return to your role as an analyst at CableMax. Early into your tenure, you realized the idea for the For You homepage came from the engineers on the team. This project was a grassroots effort that wasn't reflected in the company's product roadmap. Sometimes the best ideas come from the individuals on the ground floor building and designing the product. With A/B testing, you can take big bets, even when the odds seem against you, and turn them into a success story.

Now that we've detailed why A/B testing is beneficial for not just your users and the product but also your team, let's apply how A/B testing can empower your team in the sidebar *Chapter Roundup: How Can A/B Testing Empower Your Team?*

Chapter Roundup: How Can A/B Testing Empower Your Team?

This book has two goals: to further your knowledge of A/B testing and encourage applying concepts from this book to your job. Let's start by brainstorming how A/B testing could empower your team. Are there assumptions you've made in the past that should have been vetted via an A/B test? Is there an opportunity to employ A/B testing in an upcoming project or an unfinished project that was postponed for fear of failing?

To assist in getting those creative analyst juices flowing, answer the following questions:

- What ideas, proposed by the team time and time again, have felt far out of reach? Could A/B testing make them more tangible?

- What features have you always wanted to build, but didn't for fear of failure? Would evaluating your feature on a smaller subset of users de-risk or reduce your fears?

- What ideas could spawn creativity, innovation, or joy if your team got the chance to work on them but may seem too complex initially? Could you take that idea, reduce its scope slightly, or build it to serve a smaller scale of users while still achieving the goal of learning if the idea is worth investing more time in?

- What obstacles are in your way as you reflect on the changes you've always wanted to build but have yet to do so? Are you concerned that key stakeholders won't buy into your team's idea? Or maybe your team itself doesn't believe in the concept? Or perhaps you fear the unknown—possibly the users themselves won't engage with the ideas? Could running more experiments break down those barriers?

Wrapping Up

We've covered all the benefits that come with A/B testing. Now it's time to leap into the *how*. How exactly do you construct an A/B test? What's needed to uncover user and product insights?

Before we shift gears, let's reiterate the benefits of testing. A/B testing can:

- Minimize the risk of failures, as you evaluate changes on a subset of users before launching the feature to 100 percent of your user base.

- Increase insights about your users—how they engage with the product and react to changes as the product evolves.

- Combat bias to create more inclusive products.

- Empower your team so anyone can test an idea regardless of their job title.

- Enable better decision-making in the future as the product evolves, given data insights from past experiments.

- Reduce the fear of failing, as there's no such thing as a failed A/B test. Even if your hypothesis was found to be false or inconclusive, you still learned something that can be applied to your next decision.

To innovate and evolve your product to meet the needs of both your users and your business, you don't need the right answer at the start but rather the means to figure out what works and makes a difference. A/B testing will certainly open the doors to understanding the impact of your changes.

Now that you're ready to jump from the *why* into the *how*, it's time we let you in on a secret about A/B testing. You actually don't need to know *every* possible aspect of this experimentation methodology to get started, but you do need to know the basic anatomy of a test. The next chapter will cover the foundational components necessary to create a successful and meaningful A/B test.

CHAPTER 2

Learn the Fundamentals of an A/B Test

A/B testing can be complex, but becoming familiar with the anatomy of an A/B test will reduce the complexity. How you structure your test will directly influence the insights you'll gain from running the test on your product.

The previous chapter focused on the benefits of A/B testing, including gaining user insights and empowering your team to try out new ideas. Now that you're familiar with the advantages of A/B testing, we'll explore the following:

- The structure of a well-defined hypothesis statement.

- The objective of different types of metrics used to measure the outcome of an experiment.

- The characteristics that define a good metric worthy of using in an A/B test.

- The sampling techniques to create test and control variants.

- The variables to ensure the experiment will detect an effect.

We'll continue with the CableMax example by working through the components of the For You A/B test by defining the anatomy of the experiment, which includes the hypothesis, criteria to allocate users to the experiment, and metrics.

By now, I know (okay, hope) you love A/B testing and want to understand how to create a well-structured experiment. This chapter will help you get there, so let's go!

Creating a Clear Hypothesis

As human beings, we communicate to relate with each other, and it's important that we can communicate clearly and effectively. With A/B testing, sharing why you're testing a change is especially important when something controversial or sensitive is up for evaluation. Any genuinely great undertaking is going to require changing some minds. Your hypothesis statement communicates what you believe will happen by introducing a change to your users so it's clear to anyone, even those who may not have the same conviction.

The hypothesis statement expresses what the A/B test seeks to evaluate. It's where you'll define what you believe will happen because of your underlying assumption of the changes made to the product. It's your key to learning, as it conveys what you want to learn. And remember, A/B testing has many benefits, but the main attraction is learning about your users and product.

Constructing a Hypothesis Statement

As with anything well used in the scientific community, there are many opinions on the syntax of a hypothesis statement. Should it start with "if" followed by "then" versus "we believe"? Or should a hypothesis include the prediction or just state what you believe to be the case about your users? Let's keep it simple. Regardless of which syntax you opt for, try to include the following:

- The outcome you're predicting will happen by evaluating the change on a subset of users.

- The definition of success or result of introducing the change.

- The reason you believe your predicted outcome will come to fruition.

Including these details in your hypothesis will ensure that anyone, and I mean *anyone*, can review it and give their opinion on whether or not they buy into the statement. With the hypothesis statement, you're setting the stage for the team's work and for stakeholders to understand the work. See the template shown on page 29.

Creating the For You A/B Test Hypothesis

Crafting the perfect hypothesis statement will become much clearer once we've practiced a bit. So let's dig back into the For You A/B test.

Hypothesis Template

We believe...	State the proposed solution. The variable that is being evaluated.
will then...	The result of introducing the change. The definition of success.
because...	Concise and clear rationale or evidence for this prediction.

First, take a look at the following analyst task in the sidebar *Analyst Task: Create a Hypothesis for the For You A/B Test.*

Analyst Task: Create a Hypothesis for the For You A/B Test

As part of your analyst role at CableMax, create a hypothesis statement that includes the three main elements:

- The solution the team implemented: the For You homepage.
- The problem that the solution is addressing: to provide a personalized experience for users to access their TV shows and movies easily.
- The criteria for evaluating the solution that was introduced from a metrics perspective: increase in consumption of content on the video product.

Use the template on page 29 to help create your statement before we reveal different variations of the For You A/B test hypothesis.

The hypothesis statement that the team launched the A/B test with is as follows:

We believe that introducing a personalized For You homepage to the video browsing experience will increase the consumption of movies and TV shows because our users will easily access content personalized just for them when compared to the non-personalized browse structure.

Clarity is essential here. When your peers or teammates don't understand what is tested or how it's evaluated, they're unlikely to buy into the results and they'll push back on launching the feature.

Comparing Your Hypothesis Statement

How did your For You A/B test hypothesis compare to the one the team launched with? How did your statement differ? Maybe you incorporated specific user groups into your hypothesis statement that would most benefit from the For You homepage, knowing the additional analysis that was conducted in *Why You Should A/B Test*. Or maybe you included the metric within the hypothesis statement, that is, video plays. If you did either of these, your hypothesis could look like the following:

We believe that introducing a personalized For You homepage will have a positive gain in video plays for the segment of users who have a high consumption of content on the product because it will enable them to quickly and easily access content personalized just for them when compared to the non-personalized browse structure.

The beauty of A/B testing is that it enables you to try out any idea on just a subset of users. If you build that culture within your organization to take big risks, there will be instances where you're evaluating a change that may be met with little interest or support. A clear, well-defined hypothesis will make it easier to advocate for your changes to stakeholders who may push back or have minimal time to understand the details. You're more likely to gain support if it's *very* clear what's being evaluated and how you'll demonstrate the impact.

Measuring the Impact of an Experiment

A metric is a data point. This data point represents something the team wants to observe and understand—for instance, clicks and impressions of images on a website. Or a metric could represent a business-oriented data point, such as revenue and subscription upsells. Metrics are the key to demonstrating the effect of your changes to the product.

Gauging an Effective Metric

When you build a solution that solves a problem, you usually hedge a bet that your solution will address the problem. How are you going to ensure that's the case? Well, with an A/B test. The metrics that are defined as part of your test configuration will help demonstrate the impact of the change to your product.

Qualities that define a good, effective metric are as follows:

- Easy to understand, preferably a single ratio, count, or rate. If your peers and teammates can't quickly interrupt the metric, then it's less likely to be accepted, so it becomes harder to advocate for when getting buy-in on test results.

- Simple to compute. The metric does not require a complex formula involving other metrics, also called a composite metric. Composite metrics are difficult to interrupt, as multiple variables are at play, and are more challenging to isolate user behavior. Always err on the side of simplicity.

- Actionable by your team. If the numbers decrease or increase, a good metric is something you know you'll want to take action on as a result. If there's a degradation, it indicates a problem, and your team will work on identifying a solution to that problem. If you find that regression of a particular metric isn't something your team acts upon, then it's a lousy metric.

- Reliable to produce. The more trust you have in the data pipeline that creates the metric, the more you increase your chances of learning how a change influences product engagement. If the data pipeline requires vast engineering infrastructure, it could delay the metric's availability or fail altogether.

These qualities are summarized in the image that follows.

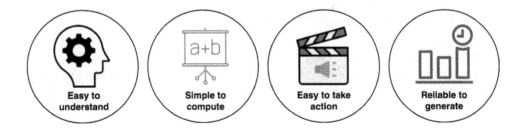

Keep these qualities in mind as we define the different types of metrics used in an A/B test.

Defining Success Metrics

Winning, or being successful, is defined by how you keep score. If you're in a new business, then maybe you keep score by the number of new customers. If you're playing soccer, you keep score by the number of times the ball passes the goal line. (Hopefully it's your opponent's goal line, not yours.)

Whether it's a business plan or a sporting event, it needs to be clear how the score is kept.

In the context of A/B testing, when your test has concluded, how will you know you prevailed and achieved the outcome you predicted? How you measure success is defined by your success metrics.

A success metric, also referred to as a primary metric, is the metric you want to move to demonstrate that the A/B test had the predicted effect. This metric (or set of metrics) gives you the insight needed to understand if you succeeded in the intended effect stated in the hypothesis.

Your success metric could signal the user has an interest in the new feature. Alternatively, it can also measure the value added from a business perspective. Defining your success metric requires you to understand what you're seeking to optimize for the change that is up for evaluation.

Let's revisit the For You A/B test. The success metric was total video play, defined by the number of TV shows and movies users on the video product watch. The team predicted that introducing a personalized For You homepage would increase video plays for the test variant compared to the control. Have a look at the next analyst task in the sidebar *Analyst Task: What Success Metric Would You Select?*

Analyst Task: What Success Metric Would You Select?

Unfortunately, the CableMax team doesn't have the right data to create the ideal metrics to measure the impact of the For You A/B test. The team had to opt for total video plays because it was a reliable metric that they could trust.

Having gained more experience as an analyst at CableMax, what other metrics would you use to evaluate the For You homepage? Is there a better, more accurate metric to determine the effect of introducing the For You homepage on the video product?

Brainstorm alternative metrics before we discuss further in Revisiting the For You A/B Test Metrics, on page 37.

Identifying Guardrail Metrics

When you make changes that optimize one metric, you might inadvertently affect another metric. With A/B testing, it's common to have trade-offs in which one metric will dip while another metric rises. How do you know if another metric has changed, whether it's a positive or negative change? You configure your test to include guardrail metrics.

Guardrail metrics, also called secondary metrics, are used to ensure that a change does not have an unintended effect, especially ones of the negative kind. These metrics are usually the ones you don't want to "mess up" while designing features that optimize other key business or product metrics.

If the A/B test demonstrates significant increases in your success metrics without hurting your guardrail metrics, then congratulations, it's a win!

If the A/B test demonstrates that a guardrail metric has dipped, alert the product or business stakeholders who care the most about the metric. Getting buy-in before launching the change to all your users would be best.

See the following table for examples of common guadrail metrics.

Metric	Description
User Retention	A metric that measures the continued use of a product by users.
Revenue	Total amount of money brought in through transactions given the product offering.
Click-through Rate (CTR)	The number of times a user clicks on an entity such as an advertisement or image divided by impressions (views of the entity).
Return Visits	A metric that measures repeated engagement by keeping track of users who visit the product more than once within a given time frame.
Weekly Active Users	A user who engages with the product at least once over a period of seven days.
Monthly Active Users	A user who engages with the product at least once within a month's time frame.
Daily Active Users	A user who engages with the product at least once a day.
Customer Lifetime Value (LTV or CLV)	An estimation of how much a business can earn, or the value of, a single user over the course of its tenure.
Pageviews	Number of times a user viewed a specific page or feature within the product.
Web Performance Speed	Metrics such as time to load or time to first byte on a website.

Table 2—Example Guardrail Metrics

Choosing the metric that should be your guardrail metric is an important step when configuring your A/B test. If your product includes purchase transactions, your guardrail metric will likely be revenue. Alternatively, retention will likely be a common guardrail metric if your product is subscription based. The guardrail metrics you choose depends on what matters to your business and product.

The For You A/B Test Guardrail Metrics

Returning to the For You A/B test, the guardrail metrics that mattered most at CableMax included:

1. Weekly active users
2. Return visitors
3. Video purchases
4. Video rentals

The first two guardrail metrics, weekly active users and return visitors, are both user-centric metrics. These metrics were selected to ensure the new For You homepage was not deterring users from the product with the new experience.

The last two metrics, video purchases and rentals, directly influence revenue and quarterly earning reports. These metrics are essential to the business.

Building user-facing products requires balancing the needs of your business and your users. The guardrail metrics used in the For You A/B test reflect this. Not every change made to the product needs to optimize key business or product metrics, but at a minimum, they should be guardrail metrics to prevent unintended regressions.

Managing Metric Trade-Offs

An A/B test can have multiple success and guardrail metrics. The metrics themselves may directly conflict with each other. For example, if you increase click-through rate (CTR), you may decrease revenue. Or results from an A/B test may suggest that one metric is flat and another metric has increased. In these cases where it's not a clear-cut "win," you're managing metric trade-offs.

When trade-offs happen, you need to involve humans. Who to talk to depends on the metric. You could ask product owners who are especially knowledgeable about the company's strategy and business goals, or data scientists who may monitor the metric over longer periods. You need to decide, with your team, if it's OK to launch a feature that increased one metric but decreased another metric.

Making trade-offs is especially relevant when comparing user engagement and engineering system metrics. User clicks on the product could increase, but the cost is that your engineering systems now have a significant increase in traffic or load. If the cost is high, you must ensure that the change evaluated in the scope of an A/B test is worth launching.

Speaking of longer timelines, data scientists can be valuable partners when quantifying metric trade-offs. For example, Y percent gain in one metric is worth X percent loss in another metric. Alternatively, you could invest time in understanding the user subgroups that would most likely be dissatisfied with a metric that saw a greater loss while optimizing another metric.

Minding Your Metrics

Picking the right metric is tough. You have many factors to consider. You'll want to include metrics that capture the impact to the overall user experience, even if you're unlikely to influence that metric. Similarly, you'll want to consider monitoring metrics important to your business stakeholders.

Accessing the data that's used to compute the metric is an equally important factor when selecting your metrics. Sometimes you'll want to perform ad hoc analysis, especially if you're questioning the test results or want to understand how your metrics impacted specific user groups, beyond the averages available in your test results. To enable ad hoc data analysis, you'll need access to analyst-friendly data sets.

The last factor to consider when selecting your metrics is the definition of the metric. When a metric is consistently computed with the same definition, you can observe how different features influence the same metric. You can gain insights into how the metric increased or decreased with each A/B test, building awareness of what changes affect the metric. If you modify how the metric is computed, then consider recomputing the metric for past tests so you have an idea of how the changes that were evaluated in the past influenced the new definition of the metric.

Let's explore metric computation further in the next section.

Establishing Baselines

If there are inconsistencies in how the metric is computed, it won't be easy to establish a baseline. A baseline is the conversation rate of the metrics before a change is made. It's your ground truth before any changes are made that could result in a lift or regression. Before starting an A/B test, you'll want to establish a baseline to get a sense of what to expect or what you're targeting to beat before your change is launched.

Let's revisit your role as an analyst at CableMax to illustrate this concept further. See the image that follows.

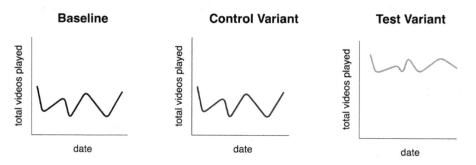

The success metric for the For You A/B test is the total number of videos played on the product. The percentage of total videos played for the control should be proportional to the baseline, the total videos played for all your users who are receiving an unchanged user experience. Similarly, you're predicting that this metric will be higher for the test variant because the For You homepage provides a personalized experience that recommends TV shows and movies based on the user's watch history.

Leveraging Proxy Metrics

As you brainstorm metrics to demonstrate the effect of your A/B test on the product, you'll likely want a metric yet to be instrumented. Instrumentation, in this context, is the logic within your product that creates the data necessary to compute user engagement metrics such as impressions, clicks, and so on. When you lack the right metric, it typically means the absence of one of the following:

- A metric instrumented at the wrong granularity such as daily aggregates instead of at the user level.

- A metric that is not *comprehensive* enough to understand user engagement.

- A metric that lacks the required *accuracy* to be trusted, especially in the scope of a success metric for an A/B test. Even the best data is only useful if it's considered trustworthy.

In a dream world, there would be no limits on what metrics to use in your A/B tests. The best metric would be decided on and then implemented. That's the dream scenario. And, like most dreams, it's not reality. Often you have to make do with what you have. This is when proxy metrics come into play.

Proxy metrics are used when your ideal metrics are not measurable or not trustworthy with the current data that's been instrumented on the product. When you defer to a proxy metric, it's important to research why movements or increases and decreases in this metric are conducive to measuring the effect.

Revisiting the For You A/B Test Metrics

With the For You test, selecting the success metric was difficult. The team at CableMax couldn't do everything they wanted to since most metrics required time from other engineering teams to build. Instead, the team decided not to gate the experiment on having the ideal metrics and opted for a proxy metric. Video play events were the most reliable data sets. This data set was also the most analyst-friendly, as you could easily query it at any granularity, such as user level, device level, variant level, and so on.

In a perfect world where metrics are easily created, you would have had an alternative set of metrics to demonstrate the effect of introducing the For You homepage on the video product. Examples of metrics that would have been better suited to evaluate the For You homepage include:

- Watch rate, which is defined as video plays divided by impressions.

- Browse time, which is defined as the amount of time a user spends browsing for a video to watch.

- For You consumption share, which is defined as the share of users' consumption that is attributed to discovering content on the For You homepage.

How does this list compare to what you had brainstormed earlier in the chapter? Considering the qualities that define a good metric on page 30, which one were you optimizing on when determining your ideal metric for the test?

If you were considering CTR, that would lend itself to deeper insight into the performance of individual recommendations, or rows, surfaced within the For You homepage. Understanding how often a user clicked on a row would enable the team to understand better which algorithm performed best. For instance, the Continue Watching row CTR versus the Recommended Movies CTR.

When it comes to data, you'll sometimes have to make compromises. It may take years for your engineering systems to reliably log impression events to compute a metric such as CTR. In cases like this, rely on proxy metrics when you don't have the exact data to create the perfect metrics.

Manifesting Your Dream Metrics

Often a conversation about metrics starts with, "Do we have a way of measuring XYZ?" Usually, the response is, "No, but I wish we had that!" There's value in noting what you don't have and making strides to get there while leveraging what you do have.

Making sure you have the right metrics, not just any metrics, is a challenge. The subtle nuance of metrics, an individual's perception of the definition of a metric, and the potential for changes in the computation of a metric, are factors to consider as you select the metrics that power your A/B test results.

Defining proper test and control variants is just as important as choosing good metrics. A good variant should represent a sample of your target audience. Because metrics are computed for each variant, the two components have a strong relationship. If your test or control variants are not defined properly, your metrics will fail to represent the target population for your product. Be mindful of this relationship in the following sections.

Defining Test and Control Variants

A variant, also called a treatment or segment, defines the subset of users from the target population. An A/B test consists of the following:

- A test variant in which users receive a different product experience or functionality that the team is looking to evaluate.

- A control variant in which users receive the existing or unchanged functionality.

Your test and control variants should consist of users who:

- Meet the requirements to be qualified for the experiment.

- Have been selected at random to prevent sampling errors or to avoid creating conclusions based on a partially represented user population.

- Have no data-logging restrictions so that product engagement and interactions are available in the data sets used to compute metrics.

Let's first explore how a user can be qualified for an experiment. To assign a user to an experiment, they need to meet predefined eligibility criteria. For example, suppose you're considering changing the onboarding process for new subscribers. In that case, the eligibility criteria would be new users of the product because existing users wouldn't engage with the onboarding process. If you make a change that only impacts certain users, such as new users, the effect would be zero if you included more tenured users who would never be exposed to the change.

We'll walk through different examples of eligibility criteria in the next section. You'll soon see that the eligibility criteria configured for an A/B test can be customized for each use case.

Illustrating Eligibility Criteria at Spotify

One company that's supreme in orchestrating A/B tests is Spotify. Let's imagine what goes on behind the curtains on this product that's used by millions.

To set the stage, the engineers at Spotify are building a new recommendations algorithm to promote podcast shows. For a user to be included in an A/B test that measures the impact of the new podcast algorithm, the eligibility criteria could be the following:

- The user must have listened to at least twenty minutes of a podcast in the past sixty days. This eligibility criterion is in place to implicitly suggest that there must be a required minimal level of podcast affinity for the user to be placed into the A/B test.

- The user must be considered active. By definition, an active user is either a monthly active user (MAU) or daily active user (DAU). This requirement filters out users who have little engagement with the product.
  If the eligibility criteria are not met, then the user will not be included in either the test or control variants of the experiment.

To illustrate further, let's look at a second example. The engineers behind the Spotify homepage have a new version of the homepage they want to evaluate. To be eligible for the experiment, users must trigger an exposure event suggesting they've engaged with the homepage. This exposure event determines which users are allocated to the test and control variants. As soon as a user has been exposed to the homepage, they're now eligible for the experiment.

Suppose you desire a deeper understanding of how Spotify orchestrates A/B testing. In that case, you can start by reading the first post in the two-part series titled "Spotify's New Experimentation Platform (Part 1)." In particular, take note of the evolution of the experimentation platform.

The team at Spotify started by building a simple platform, as detailed in the following text snippet, and then evolved as engineering limits were hit and a more sophisticated solution was needed:

ABBA as a system was quite simple. Each experiment (or rollout) mapped one to one to a feature flag, named after the experiment. When a client fetched the value of the feature flag, it got back the name of the treatment group—e.g., "Control" or "Enabled" or "Sort according to color"—anything the user decided to name the group. (Fun trivia: some users of ABBA started encoding more elaborate configurations as JSON in the group names. Life finds a way.) Every time a feature flag value was resolved, an event was logged, which fed into the exposure and results pipelines. For each experiment, only a small number of metrics were calculated. Many of these metrics were not very sensitive, leading to almost all analysis being performed manually in notebooks.[1]

As you can see, you don't need a super-complex engineering platform to start A/B testing. For instance, it's OK to start simple with your segmentation logic. It's also fine to leverage proxy metrics when you don't have the ideal metrics to start.

To get more hands-on experience in defining the criteria that shape the user variants for an experiment, have a look at the next analyst task in the sidebar *Analyst Task: Define the For You Test Eligibility Criteria*.

Analyst Task: Define the For You Test Eligibility Criteria

Now that you have a general idea of eligibility criteria, let's apply this concept to the A/B testing at CableMax. What should the eligibility criteria be for the For You A/B test? As the analyst, what criteria would you require for a user to be eligible for the experiment?

Brainstorm ideas before we continue with the following passage.

Eligibility Criteria for the For You A/B Test

Let's revisit an A/B test you're much more familiar with, the CableMax For You A/B test. The eligibility criteria for a user to be included in the test or control variant are as follows:

- The user must be considered active, defined by watching at least one video in the last thirty days.

---

1.   https://engineering.atspotify.com/2020/10/spotifys-new-experimentation-platform-part-1/

- The user must have visited the browse section of the video product in the last thirty days. The browse section is where the For You homepage is rendered on the product.

How does this list compare to what you had defined as the eligibility criteria? You may have considered a different definition of an "active" user. You could analyze the usage distribution across users and create clusters based on their consumption habits. Then use the clustered data to determine the definition of an active user. If a user falls into the higher percentile, meaning in a cluster that watches more than the average amount of content, they would be eligible for the A/B test.

You may have considered incorporating an exposure event that would trigger users into the For You A/B test. In that case, if a user was exposed to the browse experience by navigating to that particular part of the video product where the For You homepage would reside, they were eligible for the A/B test.

One pitfall to keep in mind if you leverage exposure events to trigger a user into a test is that it may be harder to generalize the effect of the change if it does not encompass a representation of the overall population. To continue with the For You example, if you were to only account for users who engaged with the browse experience, how would you know your metric gains would persist for the larger population that included users who did not meet the criteria? To prevent misleading interpretations, ensure that your results state that representation in the test and control variants was of a subset of the overall user population and shouldn't be used to generalize the impact.

Now that we have a firm grasp on defining the criteria for allocating users to a test, let's explore how randomized variants are critical to the experiment's validity.

Randomizing Users Allocated to the Experiment

How you create your test and control variants is an important step in ensuring your test results are valid. The key to determining the users allocated to the experiment is to ensure proper randomization is applied.

Why is randomization so important? First, randomizing the users will allow you to determine causal effects with high probability because your control and test variants are likely similar. Second, it eliminates statistical bias because each user has the same chance of being selected for the experiment (based on the eligibility criteria). Third, it evenly distributes users with various attributes such as location or demographics, also referred to as co-variates.

Randomizing users as they're allocated to your test is important, to say the least. If users aren't randomized into the test and control variants, you'll risk that their engagement with the product differs because they are different not because of the change introduced.

Next, we'll explore the different randomization strategies to determine the users allocated to each variant.

Choosing the Randomization Unit

To allocate users into your test and control variants, you'll need a way to sample users from the larger population.

Sampling is the logic for selecting users representing the target population to shape the variants in an experiment. The sample of users that compose the test and control variants should be *balanced similarly*, where balanced in this context refers to a similar population of users. In random sampling, every user has an equal probability of being selected from the larger population. See the following image.

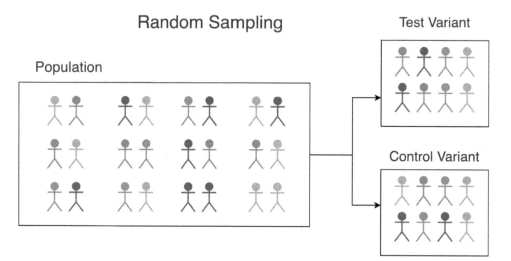

With randomization in mind, how would you split out a subset from the target population? You're spot on if your first thought is to randomize based on the user. User is a standard randomization unit, the attribute to which the randomization is applied. The most common randomization units include the following:

1. Pageview randomization: randomly assign users as they are exposed to a page on the product into a variant.

2. Session randomization: a period of activity on the product, also called a visit, in which a user will be assigned a variant for the duration of that session.

3. User randomization: based on the experiment's eligibility criteria, a user can be assigned a variant for a predefined time as they visit and engage with the product.

Regardless of which randomization unit you select, ensure it's feasible from an engineering perspective to reliably use that unit when allocating users into experiments. For instance, let's say the definition of a session on your product is up for debate. In this case, an inconsistent session definition could result in allocating the same user into multiple experiments, leading to the misattribution of metric effects.

Take a look at your next analyst task in the sidebar *Analyst Task: Define the Randomization Unit for the For You A/B Test* to illustrate the importance of selecting the right randomization unit.

Analyst Task: Define the Randomization Unit for the For You A/B Test

As the analyst at CableMax, what randomization unit would you select for the For You A/B test? As you brainstorm, remember that user, session, and pageview are the most common units.

Think about this before the answer is revealed in the following passage.

Illustrating Randomization Unit in the For You A/B Test

When you were brainstorming the ideal randomization unit to demonstrate the effectiveness of the homepage, was your first instinct to select the pageview randomization? At a glance, this would make sense because you're testing a new page layout, the For You homepage. However, after a second thought, the experience must be consistent for the user. If the For You homepage appears one visit and disappears the next visit, it could be a jarring user experience that negatively impacts metrics. In this case, user randomization is the ideal choice to provide a consistent experience on the video product.

Now that we know how to allocate users to the experiment, let's shift gears and ensure your A/B test is configured correctly.

Increasing Confidence in Your Test Results

This section gives you a starting point for the core statistical concepts used to configure an A/B test. It won't be comprehensive, but it will initiate the ideas and concepts to get you started with configuring an experiment so you can have high confidence in its results.

Configuring your A/B test correctly, such that you can have high confidence in the results, is essential. The more confident you are with your test configuration, the more confident you'll be in making a decision based on the data from the test.

Calculating Sample Size

The sample size is the number of users exposed to your A/B test. If the sample size is too small, your test results may not accurately represent how your entire user base would engage or behave, given the change is in evaluation.

The more you can observe the impact of a change, the more confident you can be in the test results. Now is the time you're likely wondering how to compute the sample size. How many users should you allocate to the experiment for the results to be deemed valid? You can use an online sample size calculator.[2] The key is to understand the following two of the variables that are required in the formula:

- The Minimum Detectable Effect (MDE), also referred to as effect size.
- The baseline conversion rate.

Your product team usually determines the MDE. How much effect do we want to see before you decide whether to launch the new feature? The MDE is the minimal improvement of your success metric that you want to be able to detect within the scope of the experiment. When defining the MDE for your A/B test, it's helpful to know the effect achieved for past tests. Knowing how previous tests achieved a given effect size for the same metric you're using to evaluate a change will give you a realistic idea of the MDE you should target.

The baseline conversion rate is the expected value for the control variant for the success metric. For a refresher on metric baselines, refer back to establishing baselines on page 36.

When unsure how large your sample size should be, the common suggestion is to add more users. The larger the variants are for an A/B test, the better.

---

2.   https://www.stat.ubc.ca/~rollin/stats/ssize/n2.html

More users mean you'll be more likely to find a significant difference, given that there is a true difference. However, it's worth noting a couple of downsides to this approach. First, assuming you do not have millions of distinct users available to test with daily, you'd have to run the test longer, to ensure more users are exposed to the new feature. Second, increasing the sample size may block other tests from launching, as fewer users would be available.

Powering Your Test

Power is the likelihood that your A/B test will detect an effect if one exists. Higher power translates to a decreased risk of faulty test results.

Your experiment needs enough users, or the correct sample size, to power your test. If your A/B test is underpowered, that doesn't mean there's no effect. However, it suggests that you didn't get enough users to measure if there was a true effect. Power is determined by the variables listed in the following table, *Cheat Sheet: Variables to Determine Power.*

Variable	Notes
The Minimum Detectable Effect (MDE)	If you increase the MDE, then it's harder to detect smaller effects.
Metric Variance	If you have two metrics that are similar in what they measure, try to select the metric with a lower variance to increase power.
Alpha	Increasing alpha means having a higher tolerance for making a false positive. If the experiment is critical to the product and you can't afford false positives, then do not increase alpha but add more users to power your test. If the p-value is less than alpha, then your results are significant.
Sample Size	A larger sample size makes it easier to achieve power.

Table 3— Cheat Sheet: Variables to Determine Power

Your A/B test needs enough participants to power your tests.

For a more in-depth starter guide on calculating power, start with this article titled "Statistical Power, Sample Sizes, and the Software to Calculate Them Easily."[3]

---

3.   https://academic.oup.com/bioscience/article/56/7/607/234386

Peeking Early at Test Results

The golden rule of A/B testing: do not take early action after peeking at your results before the experiment is over. If you look at your test results too early and stop a test when a statistically significant effect appears, you increase the likelihood of a false positive. A false positive is when you think something happened, but it really didn't—so you may say yes to launching the new feature with inaccurate data to support that decision.

To illustrate, let's say you run an experiment and take an early peek at your test data. The data suggests that the test variant outperforms the control variant by 5 percent. This is great! Then you decide to stop the experiment and launch the change that was introduced in the test variant. After a few months, you notice the metric drops by 12 percent and become suspicious. Maybe your A/B test didn't have such a positive impact. You may have had a false positive and shouldn't have ended the experiment early.

To lower the risk of false positives, ensure your test results can be deemed statistically significant. There are statistical concepts that can support this, such as defining a p-value, which is the probability of observing the estimated difference between the treatment and control variants if there were no true treatment effect. For a more exhaustive understanding of the impact of early peeking, start with this research paper titled "Peeking at A/B Tests."[4]

Summarizing the For You A/B Test

As the analyst at CableMax, you've accomplished a lot with the For You A/B test. You've created the components for a well-defined A/B test, learned more about the product, and gained user insights that the team would have yet to discover otherwise. It's been a sweet journey, so sweet that maybe you're considering adding analyst to your resume.

Now it's time to sit back and relax as we summarize what we learned from the For You A/B test.

Computing Additional Data Analysis

At first, the For You A/B test results were surprising. The success metrics resulted in a minimal lift for the test variant compared to the control. To understand why this was the case, the team further analyzed the A/B test results by identifying user subgroups and computing metrics for each subgroup.

---

4.   http://library.usc.edu.ph/ACM/KKD%202017/pdfs/p1517.pdf

With the analysis, you discovered that engagement with the For You homepage differed for specific user groups. Users who watched a lot of content on the video product watched even more content when presented the For You homepage. Alternatively, the For You homepage had little effect on users who watched minimal content on the video product.

Adapting how you interpret A/B test results will enable a deeper understanding of your change's effect on your success and guardrail metrics. If you're ever questioning the results of your experiment, remember that A/B testing tells you what happened, but it doesn't tell you why. To understand why, you'll need to conduct further analysis.

Starting Sooner Rather Than Later

The A/B testing platform at CableMax was reasonably simple. The engineering system had basic logic to randomly allocate users to the test and control variant and a few metrics that were central to the product and business.

Was it easy to add new metrics to the platform? No. If that were the case, the team would have opted for a more effective success metric. Could the team rely on proxy metrics to evaluate the For You homepage? Yes.

Don't wait until you have the perfect A/B testing platform. The sooner you start A/B testing, the sooner you'll start gaining valuable information about your users and how to evolve the testing platform in the future.

Building your A/B testing platform foreshadows *To Build or to Buy an A/B Testing Platform*, where we'll explore the advantages and disadvantages of building a homegrown A/B testing solution versus integrating with a third-party solution.

Learning the Unexpected

The original prediction for the For You homepage was that the experience would increase consumption for *all* users. However, the test results suggested it influenced users who engaged with the platform often but did not increase consumption for less active users on the video product.

With A/B testing, you often learn things you didn't even know you could learn.

Learning from Failing to Launch

The For You test wasn't perfect. It was kind of messy. Remember in *Why You Should A/B Test* when the team allocated more users to the test, but a production incident prevented the change from making it past primetime? An additional one million users were deallocated from the test until the incident was resolved the next day. During this A/B test, the team learned about the CableMax users and the engineering system's resilience or lack of resilience.

A/B testing can, unintentionally or intentionally, serve as a mechanism for evaluating your engineering systems and infrastructure.

Partnering with Analysts and Data Scientists

Your role as an analyst on the For You A/B test was clearly needed. Good thing CableMax hired you!

For example, you accomplished the following:

- Brainstormed additional metrics that would be ideal for incorporating as guardrail metrics.

- Identified attributes to derive user subgroups for further analysis.

- Crafted a clear and well-thought-out hypothesis statement.

If you want to ensure you're running a high-quality experiment, start with a metrics-driven hypothesis and consult an analytics partner about experiment design. You can lean on a data scientist or analyst to properly design tests so the effect is measured and trusted. They can help you make decisions on how to measure the success of a test, including which guardrail metrics to select and estimated effects of those metrics based on past analysis.

We've summarized the meatiest insights from the For You test. When, *not if,* you decide to take on A/B testing in your next work project, use the checklist in the sidebar, *Chapter Roundup: A/B Testing Checklist,* on page 49.

Wrapping Up

Nicely done! We've covered the basic anatomy of an A/B test. Understanding these fundamental components gives you a solid foundation to build on.

Here's what we covered:

- The structure of a well-defined, clear hypothesis statement that serves as the guiding North Star of the experiment.

- The traits that make a good metric.

- The types of metrics, including success, guardrail, and proxy metrics.

- The random sampling techniques to create the test and control variants.

Chapter Roundup: A/B Testing Checklist

Great job! The For You A/B test was a success. It's time to explore how to apply A/B testing to your next work project. Here's a checklist to get you started.

1. Identify a change to evaluate. This change could be a UX change, a new feature, or even an engineering systems migration.

2. Create the hypothesis statement. Use the hypothesis template on page 29 to create a well-defined clear statement.

3. Select your success metrics. If the metrics you initially selected aren't reliable to compute, consider proxy metrics.

4. Define the guardrail metrics for the experiment. Think about the metrics that need to be monitored but not optimized for.

5. Create test and control variants. Make sure the composition of your variants are randomly sampled from the general population.

With this checklist, you can start defining A/B tests that you would like to run beyond what you've practiced with the For You A/B test.

In the next chapter, we'll define the different types of experiments you can use to evaluate changes made to a product. You'll see how each type of A/B test will enable you to answer different questions.

CHAPTER 3

Select the Right Type of Experiment

Every day you are surrounded by choices. You could choose to cook a nourishing meal at home or order takeout. You could evaluate a new feature using A/B testing or deploy the new feature straight to production. We often make decisions that feel right at the moment without considering the long-term impact. So how do we choose the right type of A/B test? What type of A/B test will give you the product insights you need? The good news is that you have a limited number of A/B test variations to select from. Therefore, making the right decision only requires knowing what's possible.

In this chapter, we'll explore the different types of A/B tests. Specifically, this chapter includes the following:

- The deciding factors for when to select non-inferiority, equivalence, and superiority A/B tests.

- The varying holdback strategies to demonstrate long-term impact.

- The common use cases that each type of A/B test best serves.

You'll practice what you learned in the previous chapter by creating hypothesis statements, defining variants, and selecting metrics for each type of A/B test. So, most of what you'll see will be familiar to you, just applied in a slightly different way. All right, let's get into it!

Illustrating Experimentation in the Medical Industry

In its simplest form, A/B testing compares two versions and measures the difference with metrics. You give version A to one group of users, compare it to users that receive version B, and then demonstrate with data the performance comparisons. Simple as that, right?

In fact, variations of this form of testing have been well-utilized in fields that predate the tech industry. Evaluating a solution to a problem and comparing it to a control has roots in the medical field. Let's consider clinical trials as an example.

Clinical trials assess the effectiveness of a new treatment. The structure of a clinical trial is similar to an A/B test. Each has metrics, user groups composing the variants, eligibility criteria, and a hypothesis statement. Depending on the clinical trial phase, there's even a control group in the form of a placebo or alternative treatment.

As shown in the following image, the process to bring a new drug to market is similar to a product development life cycle that incorporates A/B testing.

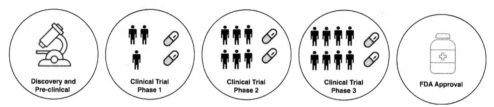

The goal of a clinical trial could be to determine whether a new medication is as good as another or better. Alternatively, the goal could be to measure if the effectiveness of a treatment is the same when comparing different dosage levels. As you'll soon see, there are A/B tests that you can select with similar intent to measure if a change is as good as the control experience, the same, or better.

This is all to say, regardless of the industry, the type of test you choose will determine the types of conclusions that can be drawn.

Defining the Superiority A/B Test

A superiority test is the type of experiment you usually select when implementing a new feature if the goal is to demonstrate that the new version performs better than another version or is *superior* to the control. When you're aiming to understand which version produces the maximal impact on a metric, choose a superiority test.

The CableMax For You A/B test in *Why You Should A/B Test* and *Learn the Fundamentals of an A/B Test* is a good example of a superiority test. The For You homepage was introduced to increase engagement compared to the control experience. The goal was not to be equivalent or almost as good, but better, significantly better, than the unpersonalized experience. We'll return to

CableMax further in this chapter, but for now, let's take a short break and go back in time to the year 2020 for an interesting A/B test at Twitter.

Experimenting with Image Presentation on Twitter

Have you ever posted an image on Twitter or scrolled through your home feed wondering how or why certain images look the way they do? If so, you're not alone. In late 2020, social media users of the platform noticed potential algorithmic biases that did not "serve all people equitably."

Specifically, users observed race bias when an image included multiple races. The algorithm favored light-skinned individuals over dark-skinned individuals, cropping out the dark-skinned individual when presenting the cropped image on the app. If a photo included two humans, one light-skinned and one dark-skinned, the algorithm would crop out the dark-skinned human from the image presented within the tweet preview. A user would have to take extra steps, clicking on the photo directly, to see both humans in the full-size image form.

To mitigate this issue in early 2021, Twitter ran an experiment to demonstrate that the new version for presenting images more accurately previewed how it will appear within tweets on the product. Twitter decided to revisit this logic for two reasons. First, the cropped images needed to provide a preview of the user's tweet accurately. Second, the image cropping algorithm could introduce serious representation harm by choosing one person over the other on a social media platform millions of humans use worldwide.

We'll use this Twitter A/B test to practice defining the structure of an experiment. Although the test configuration and results are not publicly available, let's assume the goal of this experiment is for the test variant to outperform the control.

The image shown on page 54 can be used as a basic illustration of the Twitter user experience to illustrate the intent of the test.

Specifically, you'll notice the following:

- The mobile phone on the right represents the test experience. Users in the test variant saw an uncropped preview of the image in which the photo itself is presented in its entirety, two figures included.

- The mobile phone on the left represents the control experience. The photo is cropped, so the dark-colored figure is not present in the preview image.

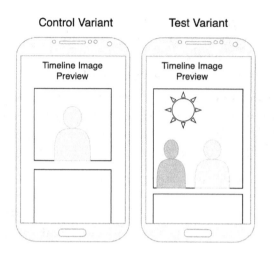

Let's pause for a moment and take what you've learned from *Learn the Fundamentals of an A/B Test* and apply it to the Twitter A/B test. Have a look at the sidebar *Analyst Task: Define the Core Elements for the Twitter A/B Test*.

Analyst Task: Define the Core Elements for the Twitter A/B Test

Brainstorm the following fundamental components to configure the Twitter A/B test before details are discussed further in the next section.

- Define a hypothesis statement for this A/B test.
- Define the eligibility criteria for variants.
- Select metrics to evaluate the performance of the experiment.

In addition to the A/B test, Twitter conducted a detailed analysis to understand better the fairness and potential harm of the image cropping algorithm. An excerpt in Twitter's Engineering blog titled "Sharing learnings about our image cropping algorithm" states:

One of our conclusions is that not everything on Twitter is a good candidate for an algorithm, and in this case, how to crop an image is a decision best made by people.

In March, we began testing a new way to display standard aspect ratio photos in full on iOS and Android—meaning without the saliency algorithm crop. The goal of this was to give people more control over how their images appear while also improving the experience of people seeing the images in their timeline.[1]

---

1.   https://blog.twitter.com/engineering/en_us/topics/insights/2021/sharing-learnings-about-our-image-cropping-algorithm

Creating a product in the hands of millions of users and evolving that product isn't easy. Mistakes happen. Learn from them. Iterate and improve. This A/B test is a great example of a company that did just that and then some, including:

- Taking responsibility for its features when user feedback suggests that the current implementation could be more optimal for everyone.

- Understanding what users want and need from the product.

- Revisiting past decisions and evaluating the impact of those decisions.

- Leveraging A/B testing to evaluate a more fair and less harmful solution.

- Forgoing the initial product requirements to display more tweets at once to provide the user with an unbiased and unaltered representation of an image.

Now let's follow up on the most recent analyst task, *Analyst Task: Define the Core Elements for the Twitter A/B Test*, and discuss the structure of the Twitter A/B test.

Applying Your Knowledge to the Twitter A/B Test

What would the hypothesis statement be for the Twitter A/B test? Although the exact configuration of the Twitter A/B test is not public, it's likely to have had a hypothesis statement that is similar to the following:

We believe that presenting the image in its original form will better align with users' expectations on how their images will appear on Twitter and mitigate risks of representational harm compared to the probabilistic machine learning solution.

Better yet, are you considering excluding representational harm in your hypothesis because it's unclear how that could be measured? That's a fair and reasonable point and would prompt a hypothesis statement similar to the following:

If we display the original image, it will then better preserve user agency because it aligns with what the user decided to upload in the first place, giving the control entirely to the user when compared to a machine learning image-cropping solution.

As with any other A/B test, you'll need to create a test and control variant. How would you define the eligibility criteria for the experiment? A few possibilities that come to mind are the following:

- Users who have an affinity for engaging with tweets containing images.
- Users who have a history of authoring tweets that include images.
- Users who span a broad range of demographics, gender identities, and countries, so the A/B test captures the target population and not the most predominant user base.

When you brainstormed the eligibility criteria, did you consider incorporating only users exposed to the Twitter timeline? If so, this could impact experiment analysis in a good way. By only incorporating users who would be exposed to the change in your variants, you are reducing noise and increasing statistical power.

As for metrics, we could assume Twitter would steer toward engagement-oriented metrics, using product features to measure how a user interacted with the change. Examples of these could include engagement signals such as likes, follows, and clicks that could equate to a product engagement metric. Or the click-through rate of tweets with images included. A metric could measure how frequently a user viewing tweets with images will engage or click on the image to go beyond the preview presentation.

If you're curious and would like to read further on Twitter's image cropping algorithm and the metrics used to measure fairness, then check out the paper by Kyra Yee, Uthaipon Tantipongpipat, and Shubhanshu Mishra titled "Image Cropping on Twitter: Fairness Metrics, their Limitations, and the Importance of Representation, Design, and Agency." In their research, they highlight the critical need to evaluate changes made to a product, especially when examining those products that can introduce representational harm, by stating the following:

Additionally, they underscore the highly contextual nature of representational harm (23); not all exposure is positive (as in the case of surveillance technology or stereotyping, for example), and representational harm provides a unique challenge to marginalized communities who have faced repeated challenges to maintaining their privacy and in advocating for positive representations in the media. Although representational harm is difficult to formalize due to its cultural specificity, it is crucial to address since it is commonly the root of disparate impact in resource allocation (20, 23). For instance, ads on search results of names perceived as Black are more likely to yield results about arrest records, which can affect people's ability to secure a job.[2]

---

2.   https://arxiv.org/abs/2105.08667

When you build products that are in the hands of users, it's your responsibility to ensure the product does not introduce representational harm. To ensure this is the case, you can use A/B testing as a strategy to fend off biases in the user experience.

Nicely done! You've practiced defining the anatomy of a real-world A/B test. Let's continue by exploring the cases when a superiority A/B test may not be the best approach.

Determining When Superiority A/B Tests Aren't a Good Fit

For some scenarios, your goal may not require that a change is better than the control. You may want to demonstrate that a change to the product is equal to the control or slightly inferior. When you're considering whether an experiment should be of the superiority type, ask yourself:

- Do you need to measure if a change equals the control experience?
- Do you want to demonstrate that the new version of a feature is almost as good or just marginally worse than the control?

If your answer is yes to the preceding questions, then a superiority A/B test is not the proper experiment for your use case. Let's explore examples in which this could be the case.

Introducing the Non-inferiority A/B Test

At this point, we love testing things. We love learning. We love proving that a new feature is better than the existing user experience. But sometimes, we may not need to demonstrate that something is better than the control but rather that something is minimally worse or as good as it. In these cases, the non-inferiority test is the best approach.

For a non-inferiority A/B test, you can conclude that your change did not worsen a key product or business metric more than a predefined level. The goal is to learn whether the change is performing equal to or slightly worse than the existing, unchanged control experience. Here, slightly worse is a specific margin that defines the inferior threshold.

To illustrate this type of A/B test, here are practical use cases for selecting a non-inferiority A/B test:

- When seeking to evaluate changes that are cosmetically the same from the user's perspective but under the hood, the engineering systems that orchestrate the output differ.

- When gauging if a cheaper-to-implement solution from an engineering perspective can perform almost as well or not meaningfully worse than the current control implementation, which is more costly.

- When making small changes, such as slightly modifying the copy of a text or an image rendered on the product.

- When migrating to a new engineering system. For instance, the migration will proceed unless you see a dip in key metrics larger than a certain margin deemed acceptable.

- When making changes that reduce tech debt and wanting to ensure the experience for the user has not degraded.

Detailing the Non-inferiority A/B Test

It's worth explaining two concepts that are key to the non-inferiority test:

- A null hypothesis states no meaningful difference between the test and control variants.

- A non-inferiority margin, also called limit, is the tolerance for a negative or relative difference in which you consider the performance of the test and control variants to be the same.

Recall from *Learn the Fundamentals of an A/B Test* that a traditional hypothesis is a statement formed by assumptions that the A/B test aims to evaluate. The hope for a superiority test is that the assumption made as part of the hypothesis will result in statistically significant gains when comparing the success metrics for the test and control variants. A null hypothesis is also a statement, but it differs in that it suggests no significant difference between the variants receiving differing experiences or versions of a product.

Now you might be asking what does "no significant difference" mean? The non-inferiority margin defines what a significant difference is. Even if a new solution is worse than the control by the non-inferiority margin, the changes that were up for evaluation can continue past the A/B test phase.

Defining the Non-inferiority Margin

If you want to test that a change is no worse than the control experience, you'll need a definition of "no worse." This is where the non-inferior margin comes into play.

To define the non-inferiority margin, start by asking your product and business stakeholders the following questions:

1. What negative change in the metric is acceptable?

2. What change in a metric would you consider to be so small that it is practically the same as the control experience?

3. What downside or risk are you willing to accept?

Once you know what your stakeholders expect, work with your data scientists to translate to a margin so you can make informed decisions. A data scientist will be able to help you define what margin is feasible from a statistical power perspective. We'll discuss statistical significance in *Interface with Data and Visualizing Results*.

Testing Cost Optimizations to Illustrate the Non-inferiority A/B Test

Let's explore an all-too-relatable scenario to illustrate a use case for a non-inferiority test.

As an analyst at CableMax, you're working with a team whose mission is to create recommendations that predict the movie a user will likely purchase on the video product. The team has implemented a machine learning model that predicts what a user is most likely to buy by using their watch and purchase history data sets as an input to the model.

Training the machine learning model requires aggregating a user's all-time purchases, from their first purchase on the video product to the current day. Can you imagine how large these data sets can get? A user could have an extreme affinity for the product, buying movies weekly for the past ten years—great for business—but not so great for data storage costs.

Speaking of storage cost, the budget police are aware of the cost the machine learning model has accrued. They've shared a graph suggesting the team spends a ton of money on storage infrastructure in the Amazon Web Service (AWS) public cloud provider.

Mounting pressure to reduce costs leads the team to seek optimizations. And they ask you to help them evaluate these optimization changes via an A/B test. Clear your calendar—there's work to be done!

First, let's iron out the details for the optimizations to reduce cost. What data set would you first attempt to refine or minimize to reduce the cost of computing these recommendations? You're spot on if you're thinking of the all-time purchases data set. Instead of all-time purchases, the model could train with the past thirteen months. Opting for thirteen months instead of twelve months gives you the additional month to account for purchases the user made this time last year—taking into account seasonality.

The cheaper implementation that uses a smaller data set, thirteen months, will be evaluated against the control, the machine learning model trained on the all-time purchases data set. Now the control and test experiences are defined, you can start drafting the A/B test specifications.

But before we begin drafting, let's pause for your next analyst task in the sidebar *Analyst Task: Non-inferiority A/B Test Example*.

Analyst Task: Non-inferiority A/B Test Example

Take a moment to brainstorm a few of the fundamental components detailed in *Learn the Fundamentals of an A/B Test* for this A/B test. Remember, the objective of the non-inferiority test is to demonstrate that the cheaper implementation is not meaningfully worse than the existing, more expensive implementation. Consider the following questions:

1. What would a clear hypothesis statement look like for this non-inferiority test?

2. What would the success metrics be?

3. What would the guardrail metrics be?

You'll soon see the definition of these components in the following passage.

For any A/B test you decide to run, the anatomy of the test is the same. In the case of the non-inferiority example, let's start with the hypothesis statement. The goal is to conclude that the cheaper machine learning model is not performing meaningfully worse than the control.

With that in mind, your hypothesis statement could look something like this:

We believe that training the machine learning model on a smaller purchases data set will be sufficient, with no significant difference in producing recommendations compared to the machine learning model trained on the all-time purchases data set.

Would you want to incorporate that you're optimizing AWS cost savings in the hypothesis statement? If so, then an alternative version of the hypothesis statement could be the following:

We believe that training the machine learning model on a smaller purchases data set will reduce AWS's infrastructure cost and be sufficient, with no significant difference in producing recommendations compared to the machine learning model trained on the all-time purchases data set.

It's worth considering leaving that detail out as it distracts from the experiment's ultimate goal. You already know that AWS storage cost is much lower in the test version of the model. Storing thirteen months of data versus all-time data meets the cost optimization goal. It's not *really* something you're looking to analyze. However, you want to conclude that the change did not worsen product metrics more than a predefined level, which is what the A/B test seeks to prove. Let's stick with the first hypothesis statement that excluded cost savings.

Next, let's define metrics for the A/B test. It would be optimal to incorporate metrics representing the user experience and business impact. For example, you could choose the following success metrics:

- Click-through rate: clicks divided by impressions.
- Purchase rate: purchases divided by impressions.

Should the A/B test include a success metric that measures the AWS cost reduction goal? AWS cost is not what this test intends to validate, but it is something you want to keep an eye on. How about instead of configuring AWS cost as a success metric, you configure it as a guardrail metric? That way, if AWS costs increase for the test variant's machine learning model, you'll be well aware and possibly decide not to roll out the change.

The last key detail is to define what it means for the test experience to be "sufficient, with no significant difference." Computing the non-inferiority margin requires a combination of domain judgment and statistical reasoning. Because this is a hypothetical A/B test to demonstrate a use case in which a test version should be as good as the control or marginally worse, let's assume that this margin is 1 percent. This means that the success metrics cannot be more than 1 percent worse compared to the control to conclude that your hypothesis statement is true. And the hypothesis is still true if the test version is better, even though it's a non-inferiority test.

Phew, you did a great job configuring the non-inferiority A/B test! Now let's fast forward a bit. Let's say the A/B test goes live. You observe that the new cheaper machine learning model is no more than 1 percent worse than the control. You share these results with your dear friends, the budget police, to showcase that you've succeeded in reducing the cost of training the machine learning model while maintaining the quality of the recommendation. High five!

Opting for an Equivalence A/B Test

The name says it all. An equivalence A/B test aims to conclude that two versions are the same or have no meaningful differences.

Let's take a second to highlight the differences between equivalence and non-inferiority A/B tests. For a non-inferiority test, the goal is to prove that version A is as good as version B. However, suppose version B is worse to some degree than version A. In that case, the inferiority test will still result in a positive outcome. In contrast, an equivalence test's objective is to prove that version A is the same as version B and that version B is the same as version A.

The beauty of the equivalence A/B test is that it pushes you to identify what change in your success metric you would consider essentially equivalent to your control. Then you can define what side effects or behind-the-scenes optimizations or improvements make the new version worth pursuing, given they're equivalent from the success metrics point of view.

In this next section, you'll see an example of how an equivalence A/B test can be applied to evaluate engineering migrations.

Evaluating Platform Migrations to Illustrate Equivalence Tests

Not all engineering teams have direct touchpoints with users. For instance, a platform team's goal is to enable product engineering teams to deliver features to the end user. Infrastructure, developer tools, and data engineering teams that build common data sets are all examples of products created by platform teams for internal use.

Just because platform engineering teams are farther down the stack doesn't mean they can't use A/B testing to evaluate changes. To drive this point home, let's revisit your role as an analyst at CableMax. This time, you're collaborating with the data engineering team that creates common data sets used by teams that build machine learning models, similar to the use case for the non-inferiority test earlier in the chapter.

Like most platform engineering teams, you realize that, once again, the team has a migration on its hands. Nobody likes migrations, yet here you are, another day, another migration to support. The team has to upgrade the data pipelines to a new framework, as the current framework will soon be deprecated. This will hopefully be just a lift and shift.

Let's proceed with this migration. First, the data engineers will translate the pipeline code from Scala to Python. The next step is to validate the translation by manually comparing the outputs from the original data pipeline to the new version. The new version of the data pipeline should produce the same data set as the original implementation.

Your intuition starts to kick in when the team walks you through their validation process. You begin to have a vague but strong sense that manually comparing data sets may leave room for human error. What can go wrong, will go wrong. The team should be more thorough. Some questions now come to mind:

- What if a bug is introduced that's only noticed by teams using the data set that are closer to the user, upstream from the data engineering team?

- What if bias is introduced into the data set?

- What if data is dropped in the new pipeline that goes unnoticed?

The best way to answer these questions is to A/B test the output of the data pipeline migration. However, it's not straightforward since the team doesn't have a direct touchpoint with the end user experience. It would help if you had a use case that utilizes the output of the migrated data pipelines.

You have to be creative here and lean into your relationships with partner teams. Specifically, you have to ask the teams upstream of the platform, closer to the user, to integrate an existing feature that's using this data set, but with the new data set so it can be compared to the feature that's relying on the soon-to-be-deprecated data set.

When asking your partner teams for this favor, you could influence them by creating the A/B test specifications ahead of time. Doing some heavy lifting is always helpful, especially when asking for a favor. You've already practiced defining a hypothesis for the superiority and non-inferiority A/B test examples in this chapter, so let's do the same for this equivalence A/B test.

We'll step back into your role as analyst for this next task in the sidebar *Analyst Task: Write a Hypothesis Statement for the Equivalence A/B Test.*

Analyst Task: Write a Hypothesis Statement for the Equivalence A/B Test

Before reading the next passage, create a hypothesis statement for this equivalence A/B test. Given that you're on a platform team and setting up the test for a product engineering team, it's OK to have placeholders for unknown details.

As you write the hypothesis statement, remember the goal of an equivalence A/B test is to demonstrate that a change is not better or worse but instead equal to the control implementation.

Here's an example hypothesis statement to evaluate the changes made in the migration:

We believe that VERSION A of a feature will have no meaningful difference when compared to VERSION B, the control, because they're nearly similar in implementation and therefore should have no effect on KEY USER SUCCESS METRIC.

How does this compare to the hypothesis statement you created? Did you incorporate details specific to the data pipeline migration into the hypothesis statement? The data migration should be transparent to upstream teams that use the data sets. Suppose you're optimizing on having a clear and concise hypothesis that focuses on the outcome, not the behind-the-scenes details unseen in the user experience. In that case, excluding the migration-specific details is the right approach.

All's well that ends well. Let's assume that your partner team's A/B test is successful. The test results concluded that VERSION A of a feature and VERSION B, the control, were equivalent. The team can sleep easier knowing this migration was properly validated with an A/B test, minimizing everyone's fears of introducing a change that could negatively impact the user experience.

Evaluating an Architectural Change to the For You Homepage

Let's come back to A/B testing on CableMax's video product. Time has passed since the initial For You homepage launch. The team has a new version to evaluate. Well, it's not a new version from the user's perspective. The change should be transparent to the user as it's an architecture change. See the image on page 65.

The goal of the new architecture is to decouple storing a user's watch history from a user's purchase history. The data was stored in the same watch history cache in the original architecture. From a product standpoint, nothing has changed. However, this architecture will enable future product features now that it's easier to integrate new data sets. Let's think about this further in the sidebar *Analyst Task: What Type of A/B Test Would Be Best?*

Analyst Task: What Type of A/B Test Would Be Best?

What type of A/B test would demonstrate that this engineering architecture does not degrade the user experience? Contemplate this before we discuss the A/B testing details in the following passage.

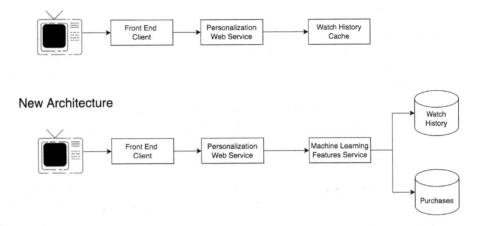

Let's start with defining the metric for this A/B test. It would make sense to continue to use the same metric, video plays, from the original For You A/B Test. You've already established a baseline value for this metric, so interrupting the test results should be fairly easy. Now that the metric is defined, the hypothesis statement can be crafted. Consider the following:

We want to learn if the new engineering architecture, which decouples the purchase data from the watch data when accessed on the user request path, did not worsen video plays more than the predefined level of 0.1 percent.

Knowing the metric and hypothesis, do you think this architecture change should be evaluated with a non-inferiority, superiority, or equivalence test? You can immediately rule out superiority since this change is not expected to positively impact the video plays metric. If you selected non-inferiority, then you're spot on! With this A/B test, you want to conclude that the new architecture doesn't degrade the most important metric, video plays, by more than 0.1 percent compared to the control. If the test detects a negative impact, the architecture change will not proceed forward without identifying and addressing the root cause.

Applying Non-inferiority and Equivalence Testing in the Medical Industry

If you're interested in how non-inferiority and equivalence tests are applied within industries other than software, read the paper authored by Laura Flight and Steven. A. Julious that's titled, "Practical guide to sample size calculations: non-inferiority and equivalence trials."

The paper explores examples of how non-inferiority tests and equivalence tests are applied in the medical industry, specifically clinical trials, as seen in the following excerpt:

...once an existing therapy has been established, it may no longer be ethical to undertake placebo controlled trials. Instead, active-controlled trials can be conducted where a new treatment is compared with an established treatment with the objective of demonstrating that the new treatment is non-inferior. For certain trials, the objective therefore is not to demonstrate that a new treatment is superior to placebo or equivalent to an established treatment but rather to demonstrate that a given treatment is clinically not inferior or no worse compared with another.[3]

So far, the examples have been designed with specific product or platform decisions in mind and are usually created to optimize short-term product metrics. Next, we'll explore how to measure the long-term impact of changes made to a product.

Validating Longer-Term Impact with Holdbacks

Usually, we want to retain results as quickly as possible. However, sometimes we need more time to demonstrate the longer-term impact of changes on business and product metrics. Or maybe we want to quantify the collective impact of all product changes made within a quarter. There are also scenarios where we want to ensure the initial results continue to trend in the same direction over a more extended period. For the insights that may not yield results as quickly, this is where long-term experiments come into play.

By opting for holdbacks and long-term experiments, you can accomplish the following:

- Measure the impact of changes on metrics, such as churn or retention, that alter at a slower rate or take longer to observe.

- Learn the relationship between your short-term product metrics and long-term business metrics in a casual manner.

- Understand the impact of multiple changes collectively, given that the holdback group has yet to be exposed to them.

- Continue to observe that the trend from the initial A/B test either maintains, improves, or degrades given the initial results.

Let's first better understand what holdback experiments entail.

---

3. https://eprints.whiterose.ac.uk/97113/8/WRRO_97113.pdf

Defining Degradation Holdbacks

If you want to evaluate a feature's impact on a longer timeline that has already been launched to most users, then you should select the degradation holdback, also called holdback.

For a degradation holdback, most users will receive the feature. At the same time, the feature is unavailable for a small percentage, the holdback group. Reasons to run a degradation holdback include the following:

- If you're comfortable removing the feature from the experience for the set of users in the holdback group and potentially degrading the experience if that feature is key to the product experience for a longer time period.

- If you require the flexibility to select which combination of features to remove for your evaluation.

- If you want to know the impact of a feature on certain key business metrics that take longer to observe, such as three to six months.

Using a Degradation Holdback for the For You Homepage

To further illustrate when to use degradation holdbacks, let's return to the For You homepage at CableMax.

It's unclear what the long-term impact is of the For You homepage on the video product. To attain this insight, the For You homepage would be the perfect candidate for a degradation holdback.

The For You homepage was a significant change to the CableMax video product. It's important to use a degradation holdback to mitigate the risk of unintended effects by monitoring key metrics such as long-term retention and video consumption. By employing a degradation holdback, you'll be able to answer the following questions:

- Will the initially observed increase in consumption persist over time?

- Will other user cohorts benefit from the For You homepage that may have taken more time to become familiar with the feature?

- Will the For You homepage influence retention, whether positive or negative?

Knowing how the For You homepage affects metrics that take longer to observe, such as retention and churn, can also influence future changes to the video product. Suppose the results of the long-term experiment suggest that the For You homepage has a positive influence on user retention. In that case, the team could further prioritize similar innovations to improve user retention. It's a great example of when to use a degradation holdback, leading us to define when not to use this type of long-term experiment.

Clarifying When Not to Use a Degradation Holdback Test

You should not choose a degradation holdback A/B test if your feature is already available for your entire user base and removing the feature for existing users to create the holdback group results in disorientation with the product experience. This could be the case for features or changes that are highly visible on the product.

For example, think of common websites you visit on a daily basis and pick one to use for this exercise. For instance, websites that you might visit daily could be google.com or youtube.com.

Now think of removing the homepage or landing page from the website for A/B testing purposes. How would people behave or interact with the site if the homepage were missing? What would you do if you visited the site and realized the homepage was unavailable? Suppose the homepage were missing from google.com. In that case, some people may think their computer's malware protection software failed, causing a virus to seep its way through their browser history, one website at a time, modifying the CSS rendered. Or maybe they would restart their computer, over and over again, until google.com was restored to its original homepage.

The effect of removing a prominent feature would likely outweigh any insights you could gather if you launched a degradation holdback A/B test—unless there was a workaround that would alleviate this concern, which you'll soon see in the next section.

Leveraging the Power of New Users

A super-secret workaround if you want to implement a degradation holdback test for a highly visible feature (not so secret now) is to alter the eligibility criteria for the holdback user group to specify only *new users*. This would avoid the disorientation effect, as new users have yet to engage with the feature that's removed.

Another benefit of incorporating new users into the test and control variants is combating the Hawthorne effect or "newness" bias. Let's say a new feature is introduced, and longer tenure or existing users' interests are piqued. So, they click everywhere, over-indexing time spent initially on the new feature. This wouldn't be the case for new users who are unaware that a feature is new. New users are more likely to be less sensitive to product changes than existing users because existing users have created habits because they're more familiar with the product.

Utilizing Long-Term Cumulative Holdbacks

Long-term cumulative holdbacks are not your average A/B test. This type of A/B test is way more comprehensive, consisting of not just one or two, but potentially three or more features up for evaluation at once.

A long-term cumulative holdback is similar to a long-term degradation holdback, but instead of selecting a feature to remove from the experience, the goal is to determine the impact of the cumulative product changes from a given time period—such as quarterly. This test design involves holding back a small portion of users that will not get exposed to any product changes made over a given period of time with the intent of observing the impact of all successful changes in aggregate. Let's highlight a few terms that are key to the implementation of a cumulative holdback experiment before we dive deeper:

- Holdback period: the start and end date in which new features or changes occur within. If we use a quarter as an example, a change must occur within the quarter for it to be included in the cumulative holdback test.

- Static experience: an unchanged version of the product for the duration of the holdback period.

- Holdback group: the subset of users who will receive the static experience during the holdback period.

- Evaluation period: the time after the holdback period where an A/B test is executed. The test and control variants are composed of the holdback group, where half of the users receive all the updates, at once, to the product during the holdback period. The control variant consists of the other half of the holdback group and will continue to remain held back.

The idea here is to exclude a small percentage of users, the holdback group, from receiving all product changes for a predetermined time, the holdback period. A static experience will be maintained for the users in the holdback group as new features are tested and launched into production. At the end of the holdback period, such as the end of the quarter, you'll then kick off an A/B test where all the successful changes from the quarter are captured within the variant that the test variant receives. The holdback group will be split into a test and control variant, where the test receives all of the successful changes made within the quarter and the control receives the static experience. See the following example cumulative holdback timeline to measure quarterly impact.

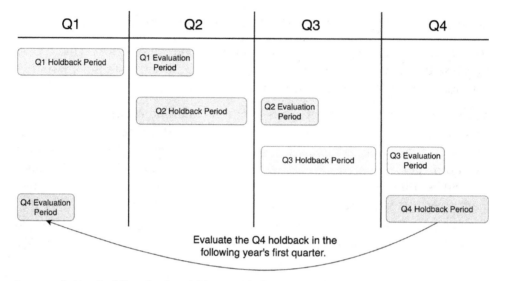

A cumulative holdback should be used if you're seeking to learn the following:

- The impact of your team's output for a given quarter or specific date range.

- The impact, in aggregate, of multiple changes on a product experience that rolls up to a larger product vision.

- The impact of a set of changes on business metrics that take place at a slower rate, such as retention.

A cumulative holdback should not be utilized if the following scenarios are true:

- You're seeking to evaluate the long-term impact of an individual change or feature. This is when a degradation holdback should be utilized.

- You'd like to avoid the spillover effect—when users know that other users, like their friends, are receiving features they don't have in their product experience. If this is the case, it could change user behaviors and skew or bias the test results.

- You're mindful of the engineering cost of maintaining two substantially different experiences since the holdback is not specific to one change, but changes that could span a longer timeline.

Remember, a long-term cumulative holdback aims to demonstrate the overall impact of the new features or changes that were deemed successful given their individual A/B tests from a particular time period. You'll already know the results of individual, incremental changes evaluated in isolation, with specific metrics they seek to optimize. Select a long-term cumulative holdback test to understand the combined impact of multiple new features or changes.

Planning Ahead for a Long-Term Cumulative Holdback

A cumulative holdback requires more planning than the other types of A/B tests. This planning includes the following:

- Identifying a holdback group before changes are tested and launched. These users should not receive any changes from the start of the holdback period until the cumulative holdback A/B test begins. Said otherwise, it's critical to the validity of the test that a distinct set of users is set aside and held back from any changes during the quarter.

- Assessing the feasibility of the product to maintain a static version that does not include changes made throughout the holdback period.

- Maintaining a list of the successful A/B tests or feature launches, as these changes will be included in the cumulative holdback test for the holdback group to receive for the first time. Features that didn't pass the A/B testing phase should not be incorporated into the holdback test.

These requirements are worth highlighting, as they're unique to the cumulative holdback test. Before running this type of A/B test, plan for these requirements.

Assessing Your Product Vision, Holistically

Are you sold on long-term cumulative holdbacks yet? Or are you questioning if this type of test is necessary? Well, if you're still undecided, consider this.

Let's say you have a product vision that spans six months of development work. This product vision comprises ten distinct changes. For some changes, you may use a superior test to demonstrate that the test experience is better than the control. For changes that ladder up to a bigger product strategy but may not hold up on their own, you may decide to employ a non-inferiority test. One way to tie all the changes together is with a long-term cumulative holdback test.

To run a long-term cumulative holdback, implement the following steps:

1. Define the holdback period that represents the start and end of your product vision. It could be a few weeks, a few months, or a quarter.

2. Set aside the users that will be allocated into the holdback group at the beginning of the holdback period. These users will not receive any new features or product rollouts during the holdback period.

3. Configure a static version of your product to be made available for the holdback group.

4. Run standard, shorter-term A/B tests as you would normally. These experiments evaluate individual new features or incremental changes that, in aggregate, represent the bigger-picture product roadmap.

5. Ensure that the users in the holdback group are not exposed to any A/B tests or new launches during the holdback period.

6. Run the cumulative holdback test at the end of the holdback period. The holdback group is split into a test and control variant. The test receives all the successful changes at once from the past quarter. And the control continues to receive the static experience from the beginning of the quarter, before any changes were launched.

For a visual representation of the steps outlined above, see the following timeline illustration for a long-term cumulative holdback.

The A/B tests that ran throughout the holdback period.

| Test 1 | Control 1 | Test 2 | Control 2 | Test 3 | Control 3 | Holdback group |

| No A/B Tests Ran | Test 4 | Control 4 | No A/B Tests Ran | Holdback group |

| No A/B Tests Ran | Test 5 | Control 5 | Holdback group |

| | Holdback Control | Test 1 / Test 3 / Test 4 |

Maintain a holdback group that does not receive any new changes during the holdback period.

Evaluation Period

At the end of the holdback period, kick off the cumulative holdback test. The test variant includes all the successful changes launched throughout the quarter, and the control is the static experience. The test and control variants consist of users from the holdback group.

Understanding the Cost of Long-Term Holdbacks

We spend an estimated third of our lives sleeping. So buying an expensive mattress or overpriced flannel bed sheets may initially seem like a waste. However, once the cost is correlated to how much time is spent sleeping, it's pennies in comparison. Similar to how an expensive mattress can improve one's sleep dramatically, long-term experiments may seem expensive initially but are very much worth it in the long run.

As powerful as long-term experiments are, let's recognize the big cost elephant in the room. Maintaining multiple versions of a product or feature, especially on a longer timeline, has a cost. It's easy to make mistakes when managing multiple versions of codebases or maintaining a holdback group. For example, suppose you have two versions of a machine learning model. In that case, you're supporting two training pipelines, two model deployments, and two monitoring systems. That's double the infrastructure cost, maintenance, and engineering brainpower if an incident occurs.

Despite these factors that suggest holdbacks are not worth it, there are many benefits to running long-term experiments. The benefits of running any of the variations of a long-term holdback include:

- Understanding the cumulative impact of all the features built within a date range, often quarterly, as product teams often have quarterly-driven goals.

- Knowing that the results from your smaller-scale, individual feature evaluation A/B tests either align with the holdback experiment results or suggest otherwise. You could learn that a feature performs well for the shorter-lived tests, but in a long-term holdback, the impact over time isn't what was initially observed.

- Gaining insights into the impact on longer-term business metrics, like retention or revenue.

By now, you're likely a believer, a long-term holdback believer.

Importance of Long-Term Holdbacks in Machine Learning Systems

Building machine learning systems that do exactly what they originally intended to do is very hard but not impossible. Consistently computing reliable predictions using data that is fully capable of changing over time requires the need for monitoring, that is, long-term monitoring.

Consider the example described in the paper titled "Practical Diversified Recommendations on YouTube with Determinantal Point Processes" by Mark Wilhelm, Ajith Ramanathan, Alexander Bonomo, Sagar Jain, Ed H. Chi, and Jennifer Gillenwater. The paper details the importance of long-term holdbacks, specifically in measuring the impact of the machine learning model on users that are still gaining momentum 140 days after launch, as evident in the following statement:

In the second holdback condition, a consistent set of users do not see DPP-diversified feeds. We can then observe whether DPP diversification results in a long-term improvement in user experience by observing the difference between the two holdbacks when compared to their respective control groups. As we can see in Figure 6, which shows the increase in number of users watching at least one video from the homepage against these two holdback groups, users who have been exposed to diversified feeds more often realize that they can find videos of interest on YouTube's homepage. Therefore, we can say that diversified feeds lead to increased user satisfaction in the immediate term, and that this effect becomes even more pronounced over time.[4]

The key takeaways from this paper that you can apply to your work include the following:

- Practicing long-term holdbacks for algorithm changes because they tend to result in effects that require a longer timeline to measure.

- Using long-term holdbacks when building and evolving recommendation algorithms so you can observe the effect in both directions. Sometimes small gains result in more significant improvements, or large gains erode over time into small negative gains.

Although it has already been noted that the cost of the long-term holdback is high, it is well worth it. It's especially worth it in the context of machine learning, in which the complexity of monitoring and observing changes over time is made possible by leveraging holdbacks.

Assessing When Not to Select Long-Term Experiments

Is life perfect so you have all the A/B testing capabilities of your dreams? Yes. Well, actually, no. Sometimes you can't (or shouldn't) run a long-term holdback experiment. A few scenarios where this could be the case are the following:

- If your tech stack does not support maintaining a longer-term static version of the feature or product to serve as the control.

---

4.   https://jgillenw.com/cikm2018.pdf

- If there's the possibility of a negative experience when a feature is removed for a degradation holdback test.

- If it's not possible to exclude a subset of users to form your holdback group due to engineering complexities or the A/B testing platform's segmentation logic isn't quite there yet to support it.

- If the insights gained do not justify the time and engineering effort required to configure the holdback.

An alternative to consider when long-term testing isn't feasible relies on having data scientists assist you with meta-analysis. Meta-analysis is a quantitative study that can be used to

- Assess results from multiple A/B tests or research studies to derive conclusions.

- Establish relationships between short-term metrics and long-term business metrics.

Want to learn more about meta-analysis? If so, check out how meta-analysis is applied at Netflix, and read the post titled: "Improving Experimentation Efficiency at Netflix with Meta-Analysis and Optimal Stopping."[5]

Plotting Meta-Analysis in the Medical Industry

This chapter has an unintended theme—the commonalities between A/B testing and the medical industry. Check out the paper titled "Meta-analysis in medical research" for a deeper perspective of evaluations in the medical industry. The paper identifies the value of meta-analysis when heterogeneity, variability in data from multiple experiments, is present:

Arguably, the greatest benefit of conducting meta-analysis is to examine sources of heterogeneity, if present, among studies. If heterogeneity is present, the summary measure must be interpreted with caution. When heterogeneity is present, one should question whether and how to generalize the results. Understanding sources of heterogeneity will lead to more effective targeting of prevention and treatment strategies and will result in new research topics being identified. Part of the strategy in conducting a meta-analysis is to identify factors that may be significant determinants of subpopulation analysis or covariates that may be appropriate to explore in all studies.[6]

---

5. https://netflixtechblog.com/improving-experimentation-efficiency-at-netflix-with-meta-analysis-and-optimal-stopping-d8ec290ae5be
6. https://www.ncbi.nlm.nih.gov/pmc/articles/PMC3049418/

This same sentiment portrayed in the context of the medical industry to combine results from multiple independent studies also applies to evaluating changes to user-facing products in the software industry. To improve and increase insights from your A/B test results, meta-analysis will enable you to understand better how features and changes influence subpopulations or specific user subgroups.

Tying It All Together

You've developed a sophisticated palate when it comes to A/B testing. You appreciate all the flavors beyond the standard superiority test, craving the A/B testing equivalent of caviar. Remember, the type of test you select will directly influence the user insights and conclusions you'll gain. When deciding which test to choose, use the decision tree in the diagram on page 77 to help. No pressure. It's just one of many decisions you'll make with ease as you continue to attain experience in this A/B testing world of ours.

In the following Chapter Roundup, we'll look at a few questions that can be applied to the different types of A/B tests at your job.

Chapter Roundup: What Kind of Test Will You Run?

Now that you're in tune with the various types of A/B tests, see if you can identify use cases for each type of test at your job. You may have a project on the horizon or a past product decision that would benefit from a specific type of A/B test. To assist in this brainstorming session, ask yourself the following questions:

- Is there a change that reduces tech debt, but you want to make sure that you're not degrading the product by rolling it out?

- Is there a back-end engineering change that could dramatically decrease the complexity of core product logic, but you're not sure how to demonstrate the change produces an equivalent experience for the user compared to the control (or more complex solution that's already in production)?

As you're brainstorming, use the image on page 77 to assist in determining which kind of test best serves your use case.

Wrapping Up

Well done! You now know the most common types of A/B tests. In this chapter, you've learned the following:

- Superiority tests should be used to determine the effect of a change in any direction from the control.

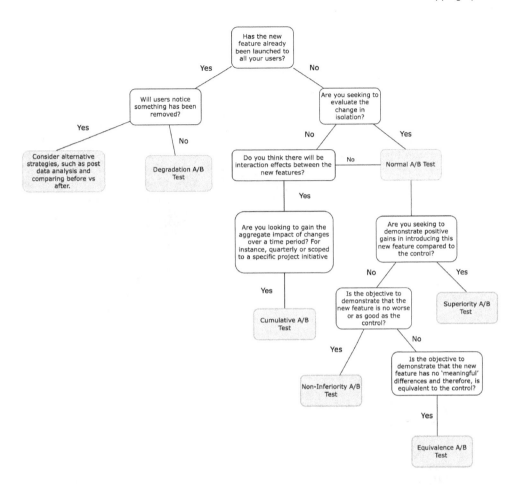

- Non-inferiority tests enable you to conclude whether a change is no worse than what is already in place, the control experience.

- Equivalence tests demonstrate whether the effect of a change is the same as the control.

- Degradation and cumulative holdbacks demonstrate the effect features have on metrics that may take longer to measure, like retention or churn rate.

In the next chapter, we'll dive into tactics to analyze the effect of A/B tests and how to ensure your test results are valid. As you'll soon see, ensuring accuracy and analyzing data to come to a conclusion is a bit more complex and totally necessary to get right.

CHAPTER 4

Interface with Data and Visualizing Results

Idea generation is easy. We could brainstorm new product ideas all day. The hard work comes when validating a new idea improves the product. A/B testing can help validate new ideas so that we're improving the product for both the users and the business. To do this, we need data to demonstrate the impact of an A/B test.

You may have noticed an important detail yet to be discussed, which is the complexities of gathering, querying, and visualizing data for your experiments while also ensuring your test configuration is valid.

The previous chapter focused on the different types of experiments. We dabbled in non-inferiority tests that seek to measure if a change is as good as the control, given a predefined margin. We learned the logistics for evaluating changes on a longer time scale by leveraging long-term holdbacks for a degradation or cumulative holdback test.

Regardless of which type of A/B test is selected, you'll need access to quality data to analyze and adequately visualize your test results. How you interface with data to create your A/B test results directly influences the A/B testing process. In this chapter, we'll explore the following:

- Common practices for storing and accessing data.

- Different types of data to create product insights and monitor the performance of an A/B test.

- Various visualizations to present the results of an A/B test.

Let's tackle the more complex and data-intensive aspects of A/B testing. Here we go!

Working with Different Types of Data

The goal of A/B testing is to observe what happens as you introduce changes to the product. To do this, you need data, a lot of data. You also need different types of data. Having different categories of data will help you with the following:

- Enable you to cross-reference and validate outcomes to increase confidence in the analysis.

- Give you the capability to monitor your engineering system health that creates the product experience.

- Provide you with a deeper, richer context for data analysis.

Let's look at the different categories of data that will create a deeper understanding of how your changes impact the product.

Defining User Engagement Data

To understand what users are up to on the product, you'll need data representing their actions and engagement. The typical path to get user engagement data is for the front end, or client side, to log events. The events will initially be raw and maybe a bit messy. When aggregated and enriched, these events can be used to understand the user's journey as they engage with the product. Examples of user engagement events include the following:

- Impressions
- Clicks
- Pageviews

When you have user engagement events such as impressions, the work to create the events is referred to as instrumentation. Let's emphasize the importance of instrumentation. To run an experiment, you'll need instrumentation within the product to create the raw events, or logs, representing how users engage with product features. Instrumentation is a crucial mechanism that will enable you to understand what the users see on the product and then do as a result of seeing a change or new feature. If you're unsure what your product should instrument, think about the actions a user can take on the product. Can a user click or scroll? How long does it take them to scroll or click something they recently saw? Implementing instrumentation will give you a richer understanding of the effect of changes introduced in an experiment.

Remember that these data points alone are usually meaningless as a unit by themselves. Any data, regardless of the type, is only valuable if you can understand it. Therefore, enriching and aggregating it to improve interpretation is key. Let's look at the data architecture at CableMax to illustrate how user engagement data can be combined with additional contexts to create a richer understanding.

Translating User Events at CableMax

Remember that users subscribe to CableMax to watch their favorite TV shows and movies on the company's flagship video product. The personalization team launched the For You homepage to help users to find their favorite content—so they spend less time looking for content and more time watching it.

When a user watches a movie, the front-end code creates an event representing that user's engagement with the product. The watch event is translated into something more meaningful that an analyst can query, as seen in the data flow in the image on page 82.

A few important details are worth noting about the flow of user engagement data in the previous image. First, did you notice the steps between the original video play event and the enriched_video_plays table that an analyst would query? When using data sets, the more steps between the origin and destination, the more error-prone it will be. Second, the enriched_video_plays table represents a best practice. If an analyst is querying the raw data directly, they're likely creating complex queries with multiple joins. It's easier to analyze the data when data sets have been transformed, cleaned, and enriched.

Enriching with Product and User Metadata

When browsing for a movie to watch on TV, do you read just the movie title, or do you tend to look for additional information, like the release year and description? This example of using metadata to add contextual information that could better inform your decisions is also applied to data that creates A/B test results.

To understand how users engage with your product, you'll need to enrich user engagement data with metadata. The two common forms of metadata that you'd typically want to enrich user engagement data with are product and user metadata.

Examples of product metadata include the following:

- Version.
- Device type.
- Information describing the content displayed on the product.

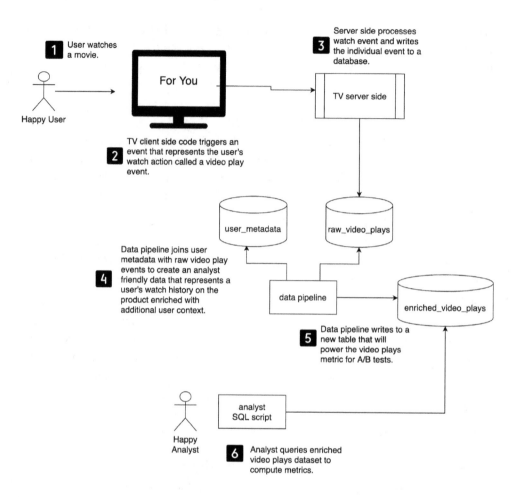

Examples of user account metadata include the following:

- Demographics such as age, location, and so on.
- Tenure on the product, such as new or existing.
- Activity level, such as daily or monthly.

Enriching raw events with metadata is one method that makes data usable. It also adds more color and context when analyzing the data sets to create your A/B test results. You never know—you may discover interesting user or product insights with the additional context overlaid on top of the user engagement data.

Next, we'll define engineering system data that can sometimes complement user engagement data.

Defining Engineering System Data

An important factor when you're evaluating changes in production is whether the underlying engineering systems are performing as expected. The most common metric to measure this is instrumenting how long it takes for a system to respond to a request. Just as you have instrumentation on the client side to understand user engagement, you should have instrumentation on the server side to understand system performance that directly influences the user experience. See the following table for engineering system metrics worthy of monitoring as you evolve and iterate on a product.

Metric	Description
Visually Complete Time	Time until all above-the-fold content has finished rendering.
Server error count	The number of responses where the status code is 500 or higher that suggest an error has occurred on the server side of the engineering architecture.
Site Availability	Percentage of total successful website visits divided by the total amount of website visits.
Web Service Latency	The total time a web service takes to respond to a request. The user's actions on the front-end side could trigger the request. If web service latency is high, then that typically results in slower user experiences.

Table 4—Engineering System Data

Another benefit of engineering system data beyond monitoring your engineering platform's health is being able to correlate this data with user engagement data. For example, let's say you're verifying that the user pageview data set is accurate and can be used as a metric in an A/B test. You notice the total web service requests is less than user pageviews. This observation might imply the following:

- A defect exists somewhere in the end-to-end data architecture. The pageview events may be logged twice, creating duplicate events every time a user visits a page on the website.

- Browser caching is in effect, and your web service isn't hit on demand for every pageview. If this is the case, it could result in stale data served to the user.

To illustrate the value of engineering system data in the context of A/B testing, let's return to your role as analyst in the sidebar *Analyst Task: Brainstorm Engineering System Data.*

Analyst Task: Brainstorm Engineering System Data

Take a look at the diagram on page 82. When a user watches a movie, a video play event is created. The video play event starts simple, in its raw form. Eventually, the event is enriched with metadata and made available in a table for analysts to query. What system data would you want to monitor that could correlate with video play events? Brainstorm a few ideas before we discuss them further in the following passage.

Illustrating the Value of System Data in Debugging A/B Test Analysis

The personalization team at CableMax thinks it's time the For You homepage got a facelift. They've designed a new UX that presents more content on a user's screen. See the following image.

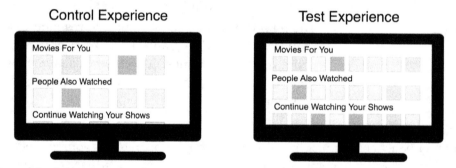

The goal of this design is simple. If the user spends less time scrolling because there's more content on the screen, they'll spend less time looking for something to watch and more time watching TV. To demonstrate whether the personalization team's theory is correct, they decide to run an A/B test.

Early test results suggest that there's a steep decrease in video plays. The team questions these data sets, so they ask you to verify if the video play events data set is accurate. What system would data be most helpful to investigate this issue? Is there an engineering systems metric that could be used to correlate with the decrease in the video plays metric? Maybe you're thinking server error count could lend itself to interesting insights. If server-side errors are high, the web service will not return all the content at once. Therefore, the decrease in video plays would be valid.

Another idea could be to monitor the latency of the web service that fetches the content displayed on the user's TV. Suppose latency is higher for the test variant compared to the control. In that case, users may not be used to waiting longer for the contents of the For You homepage to render.

As you start running more and more A/B tests, you'll find the usefulness of having system data to correlate to user engagement events.

Now that you have enough data about your product, engineering systems, and users, the second step is to ensure your data is easy to query and interrupt.

Wrangling Your Data

For data to be functional to create your A/B test results, you'll likely go through the process of wrangling the data. By definition, wrangling data is taking raw, maybe even sometimes tricky-to-parse or unstructured data and transforming it into something more usable for your data scientists and engineers. Clean, easy-to-access quality data will allow you to do the following:

- Create metrics to demonstrate the impact of your changes as part of the A/B test valuation.

- Conduct post-analysis to discover deeper insights and understand why a specific outcome was observed.

- Allocate users into your experiment variants.

See the following image that illustrates how data powers the fundamental concepts needed to run experiments on a product.

Unlike success and guardrail metrics, where you can rely on proxy metrics if your ideal metric is unavailable, there's no backup if core data sets aren't functional. Data wrangling is a complex process, especially when data is available in various formats, messy, or stored in multiple locations across your engineering ecosystem. Speaking of messy, let's explore what to do if you find yourself in a situation where your data set is unorganized and unwieldy.

Working with Messy Data

Not all messy data is created equal. Messy data can come from many locations. For instance, you could come across messy data when querying a poorly designed table in a SQL database. You may work with data from an unconventional source, like log files created initially for observability use cases. To understand what unconventional sources correlate to, let's first detail the most common *conventional* sources for data:

- SQL databases
- NoSQL databases
- Web service APIs
- File systems

If you find yourself pulling data from a source that doesn't fall into this list, you're most likely scraping from an unconventional source. And when you're scraping data from an unconventional source, the data will be messy.

Characteristics of messy data may include the following:

- Unstructured format that makes the data set challenging to read and interpret. The fields may be delimited by uncommon delimiters such as a dash or semicolon.

- Corrupt values within the data set. A portion of the file may be missing or have other low-level problems that prevent you from reading the entire data set.

- Extra characters appended to the data, such as encoded values or extra white spaces.

- Poor naming conventions that make it harder to understand the data itself.

You can combat messy data by writing code, such as SQL scripts or data pipelines, that reads the raw data, applies logic to clean it up, and then writes the transformed data set to an easily accessible location. If you perused your company's code repository, you would likely find plenty of code examples that do precisely this. Data is usually an afterthought. Sometimes it's even a last-minute scramble to confirm the data is available to compute your test results, but this doesn't have to be the case. You can prioritize data just as you would product features. Let's explore this data-first mindset in the following section.

Treating Your Data as a Product

You should treat your data as a product if you want clean and easy-to-use data. In practice, this means prioritizing and maintaining the data your product produces, similar to the product's user experience features. Here are some steps you can take to build a strong data-first culture:

- Establish data infrastructure teams that standardize collecting, aggregating, and transforming data.

- Create instrumentation within the product to understand the user's journey by logging events as to what the user sees and how they engage with the product.

- Design rigid schemas that, when necessary, evolve in a backward-compatible way.

- Assign dedicated ownership for critical data sets that power insights, metrics, and A/B test setup. These teams prioritize maintaining, producing, and monitoring the data sets.

- Define a process for communicating improvements to the data sets so that consumers can see the timeline of changes.

- Define quality, timeliness, and accuracy requirements, so that producers of the data sets are well aware of what the data consumers expect.

- Identify under-invested data sets that may fall under the "messy data" category and allocate time toward improvements.

This isn't a comprehensive data-first strategy, but it's an excellent foundation to build on. Many, if not all, of the tactics detailed depend on your organization's culture. If data is at the forefront, allocating time to your engineering roadmap to implement instrumentation on both the client and server side will be easier. Once instrumentation is available, you'll need proper monitoring and clear ownership in place to ensure the data that powers your metrics is reliable.

Next, we'll explore different data access practices, which is especially relevant given the diverse roles data plays in enabling A/B testing on a product.

Making Data Easily Accessible

How you access your data depends on where it is stored. The more accessible data is, the more likely it'll be used to create your test results and even help define your variants. The three most typical access patterns include the following:

1. Reading data from a file system or object storage service.
2. Querying data from a database.
3. Requesting data from a web service.

The first two options are the most popular methods with data scientists and analysts who prefer to run ad hoc queries with minimal code setup. Public cloud providers provide interfaces that make it easier to interact with cloud storage right from your browser. Similarly, you can download applications that provide interfaces to query databases with minimal connection configuration required. The less boilerplate code you need to write, the more time you have to analyze the data to define the effect of an A/B test. The third option, reading data from a web service, the web service acts as a layer in front of a data store. The data source is abstracted away from the consumer of the data.

When deciding where to store your data, it's helpful to reflect on the broad set of users using it. See the following table, *Roles That Engage with Data*, for an overlap in data use cases and the preferred programming languages for each role.

Role	Example Data Tasks	Preferred Language
Data Scientist	Ad hoc querying, creating dashboards, and post-test data analysis.	SQL, Python
Data Engineer	Data pipelines that process and transform data to create metrics for A/B tests.	Scala, Java, SQL
Product Manager	Ad hoc querying for deeper insights for the effect of an experiment. Creating dashboards to monitor general product metrics.	SQL
Machine Learning Engineer	Creating features and statistical analysis of machine learning models. Creating dashboards for offline and online metrics to monitor model performance.	Python

Table 5—Roles That Engage with Data

It's worth drilling into dashboards since its usage spans multiple roles. The more accessible your data is, the more likely product managers and engineers will design dashboards to monitor metrics. When creating a dashboard, you should ensure it can power decisions. If a dashboard shows a metric degradation, which causes an action to be taken by the product and engineering team, then it's helpful in making decisions. If a dashboard suggests a degradation in a metric and no one cares, then it's not very useful.

Using SQL to Query Data

If your goal is to spend minimal time setting up an environment to interact with the data, then choose a database to store the data used to enable A/B testing on your product.

The easiest and quickest gateway to data is when data is accessed using the SQL programming language, the universal database language. Most database engines are compatible with SQL code. Once you learn SQL, it will be extensible to any relational database. For instance, let's say you're familiar with Oracle databases but have recently started working with Google Cloud's (GCP) BigQuery data warehouse. SQL is standard between the two, with a few variations in syntax that can be resolved with a quick Google search.

If you're in an organization struggling to increase the adoption of data-driven tactics like A/B testing or trying to make data more accessible to all employees, regardless of how technical their role is, then invest in the infrastructure that elevates data into the easy-to-learn SQL syntax.

Next, let's explore accessing data stored in an object data storage service which is optimal if you traverse large data sets that a database may not scale well for.

Using Notebooks to Read Data

The second easiest gateway to data is through Notebooks. Notebooks are an interactive computing setup that enables data scientists, analysts, and anyone who can write code to do the following:

- Read data stored in an object storage such as GCP's GCS or AWS's S3.

- Analyze data from CSV or JSON files.

- Explore data without setting up a project, deploying the project, and so on.

- Inspect data that represents the randomly sampled users in A/B test variants.

- Visualize data from the results of an A/B test.

If you know Python, you can access petabytes of data from the ease of your browser window with a Notebook. Python is a programming language loved by many, especially those in the data science field. Pandas is a Python software library used for data manipulation and analysis. If you're eager to leverage Notebooks for A/B test analysis, then pandas may be your new best friend.

For more insights on how Netflix leverages Notebooks, beyond what was detailed here, read the post on their Engineering blog titled "Beyond Interactive: Notebook Innovation at Netflix."[1]

Creating Insights About Your Data

The first rule of using data to demonstrate the effect of changes in an A/B test is never to assume your data is always correct. To trust your test results and the experiment configuration, you'll need to trust that your data is accurate. How do you do this in practice? Simple. Create mechanisms to monitor the state and overall quality.

To start, you could manually check the data, but you know that it isn't scalable. The ideal solution would be a programmatic method that's better than human eyeballs scanning petabytes of data. There are several ways to build programmatic validation:

- Implementing null checks in fields that ultimately should have non-null values.

- Computing the general distribution of event counts. For instance, monitor the number of impression events.

- Implementing anomaly detection to catch issues earlier rather than later.

- Determining the range for values in the data set and monitoring for outliers.

- Aggregating numerical facts about data sets, such as counters on specific fields, to ensure the values are within predetermined thresholds.

The goal of deriving insights about your data is to understand the quality of information available in the data sets. Quality can be defined by the three dimensions that are detailed in the table *Data Quality Dimensions* on page 91.

The goal is to be more aware of your data and increase confidence when you're using the data to make important decisions. All data is subject to uncertainty; you can trust it if it's monitored for completeness, accuracy, and validity (the three dimensions of data quality).

---

1.   https://netflixtechblog.com/notebook-innovation-591ee3221233

Dimension	Description	Solution
Validity	Does the data have the expected values and fields? Are fields null when they shouldn't be?	Create data validation libraries that can be added to the data pipelines or scripts that produce data sets.
Accuracy	Does the data represent what it is supposed to?	Create tools that make it easy to test and define the expected state of the data.
Completeness	Is all the data present?	Create frameworks that make it easy to check if all the fields within a data set are available, such as counters.

Table 6— Data Quality Dimensions

Think about the flow of data as it moves from the source and is replicated and transformed into derivative and enriched data sets, as seen in the CableMax example on page 82. When you add quality checks, you'll want to move validation closer to the source. This will avoid error propagation more effectively and increase confidence in your A/B test results that rely on the data.

Be wary of the possibility of mistakes. Data is complex. Data in large quantities is even more complex. Depending on the person looking at the data, it can be interrupted and translated in many ways.

Next, we'll define how you can use descriptive statistics to monitor data, providing additional context about the data so that people who use it know what to expect from it.

Leveraging Descriptive Statistics to Monitor Data

Knowing you need to do something is very different from knowing how to do it. You know you need to monitor the data that fuels your A/B tests, but how? How can you summarize your data to increase trust in your test results? How can you create data about your data? One easy tactic to implement before jumping to something more complex, like anomaly detention, is to utilize descriptive statistics.

Descriptive statistics define the main features of a collection of data quantitatively. In practice, what this means is you'll be creating facts about your data that would be useful to monitor. Examples of descriptive statistics that you could apply to any data set include the following:

- Computing the minimum and maximum values for specific fields in the data set.

- Computing average values for specific fields within a data set.

- Deriving a list of possible distinct values of a data set.

- Computing the standard deviation of a field within a data set.

With descriptive statistics, the goal is to understand what your data contains to create a ground truth. Then you can use that information to monitor for deviations from the ground truth.

For a more in-depth read on descriptive and inferential statistics, which aims to understand what you can conclude from your data, check out the paper written by Zulfiqar Ali and S Bala Bhaskar titled "Basic statistical tools in research and data analysis."[2]

Assuming Is the Root of All Data Issues

It's easy to make assumptions about data. You may not think you have assumptions, but you likely do. For instance, maybe you queried a data set months ago, and since then, the data set has changed. The data volume could have increased, slowing down the time it takes to query. Or the fields you knew so well before have been updated by the engineers who manage the data pipelines.

Any assumptions made about the data you use to measure the effect of an A/B test can be risky. You may need to recalculate your test results if your interpretation of the data is inaccurate.

To illustrate this further, let's revisit the For You homepage at CableMax. The research team analyzed how the recommendations algorithm performs on the For You homepage. The analysis suggested that the algorithm has a bias for presenting English content to users who live in Germany. The team wants to guarantee the product is inclusive for all users, so they ask you to help investigate this strange algorithmic bias.

You first query the data sets the research team used to analyze their algorithm's performance. Your goal is to validate that the team is correctly interpreting the data. See the image on page 93 for the data set schemas representing video impression events and user metadata.

---

2.   https://www.ncbi.nlm.nih.gov/pmc/articles/PMC5037948/

Video_Impression	
PK	id int NOT NULL
	video_title char(50) NOT NULL
	video_description char(50)
	video_language char(10) NOT NULL
	user_id NUMBER(10) NOT NULL
	video_type char(10) NOT NULL
	ts NOT NULL default(current_timestamp)

User_Metadata	
PK	user_id int NOT NULL
	location char(10) NOT NULL
	subscription_plan char(50) NOT
	subscription_date date NOT NULL
	ts NOT NULL default(current_timestamp)
	user_name char(50) NOT NULL

When a user navigates to the For You homepage, twenty movies and TV shows are rendered on their TV. This would trigger twenty impression events that are stored in the video_impression table. If more context is needed about the user, join the video_impression table and the user_metadata table, where the join key is user_id. See the following example SQL that returns the title of the content the user saw on their TV and the user's name and location.

```
SELECT vi.video_title, um.user_name, um.location
FROM video_impression as vi
JOIN user_metadata as um
ON vi.user_id = um.user_id
```

Before we continue, let's look at your next task in the sidebar *Analyst Task: Check Your Assumptions*.

Analyst Task: Check Your Assumptions

For your next task, look at the video_impression and user_metadata tables detailed on page 93. Brainstorm assumptions you may have about the two data sets. We'll discuss this further in the following passage.

What assumptions did you make when scanning the user_metadata schema definition? You might assume the location field always adheres to ISO 3166 standards. This is actually the same assumption the research team made as well—although, it's worth noting that the location field value has no constraints that would prevent a non-ISO 3166 value. The only requirement for the location field is to have a value less than or equal to ten characters. This assumption foreshadows the next section, in which we'll find out why German users are seeing English recommendations on their For You homepage.

Illustrating the Need to Validate Assumptions

It's time to analyze the data to understand why the personalization algorithm is skewing its recommendations toward English content for users in Germany. Suppose you continue with the assumption that all values in the location field of the user_metadata data set adhere to ISO 3166 standards. In that case, users with a DE as their location would translate to Germany. To start your analysis, you run the following SQL query:

```
SELECT vi.video_language, count(*) as total_impressions_per_language
FROM video_impression as vi
JOIN user_metadata as um
ON vi.user_id = um.user_id
WHERE um.location = 'DE'
GROUP BY vi.video_language
ORDER BY total_impressions_per_language desc;
```

The SQL query returns the total impressions for users whose location equals "DE", grouped by the video's language attribute. See the following table, *Video Impressions for Users in 'de' Query Results*.

Video Language	Total Impressions by Content Language
en-US	3,312,121
es	1,271,901
fr	12,810
de	178

Table 7— Video Impressions for Users in 'de' Query Results

Based on this analysis, TV shows and movies in English receive the most impressions for users in Germany, assuming that the location field in the user_metadata table follows the ISO 3166 protocol. Now you're questioning if your original assumption on the user's location is valid; maybe the value doesn't follow ISO 3166 protocol.

To investigate further, you decide to query the engineering system logs representing the For You homepage traffic for each region. With this data, you can correlate user engagement data (impressions) with the engineering system data. See the table *Engineering System Log Results* on page 95.

With the latest analysis, it's clear that users in Delaware are engaging with the product more than users in London or Berlin. Coincidentally, Delaware's state abbreviation is DE, similar to Germany's ISO 3166 country code. Now it's even more unlikely that the location field in the user_metadata table follows the ISO 3166 country code standards. With this insight, you let the research team know that their assumption about the location field caused

Region	Total Requests by Location
Delaware	3,672,028
New York	2,829,290
London	2,029,378
Berlin	929,378

Table 8— Engineering System Log Results

an error in their analysis, and they should recompute with this newly found understanding.

This example illustrates why making assumptions about your data can lead to insights that ultimately are false. Next, we'll slightly pivot to discuss different strategies for visualizing the data from your A/B test results.

Visualizing A/B Test Results

Once your A/B test has run for its configured duration, the last step is to summarize and present your test results.

There are two options for presenting the findings from an experiment. First, you can present the results numerically in a table. Second, you can display the test results more visually with a graph. See the following examples.

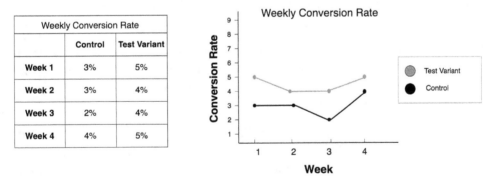

Visual representations can be easier to understand than tabular representations and sometimes even highlight insights that would be harder to see in numeric form. The following section will introduce you to visualizing your test results with graphs.

Visualizing User Engagement with Heatmaps

Heatmaps are a helpful tool to visualize numbers as colors, especially when you need to show a range of values. You should present your A/B test results with a heatmap if something has changed on your product surface and you want to overlay how that change has influenced user engagement, such as clicks or conversion rates. Heatmaps are generally intuitive, even for beginners. Additionally, heatmaps can display what is working and what is not working for the user regarding the usability or the product's information architecture. For example, if a feature on a product gets little engagement, use a heatmap to illuminate how engagement for features with X compares to features that get more user engagement.

The following image illustrates a heatmap representing the volume of video plays from specific rows within the For You homepage on CableMax's video product.

Movies For You

People Also Watched

Continue Watching Your Shows

Because You Watched Dawsons Creek

More Like You've Got Mail

TV Shows For You

The colors overlaid for each row correlates to the volume of video plays from the recommendation presented on the For You homepage. For example, the Continue Watching Your Shows row is red, which translates to more video plays compared to the green row, TV Shows For You.

Did you notice that the rows lower on the For You homepage have a lower volume of video plays? Why that is the case is unclear. Maybe users prefer to avoid scrolling to discover something to watch on TV. If that's the case, would moving the More Like You've Got Mail row to the first position increase video plays? This example illustrates the benefit of visualizing test results with a heatmap. You'll find that you're asking more questions because of how the data is presented.

Plotting Histograms

Histogram plots gather insights into how frequently specific values occur within a data set. Plotting histograms can highlight insights that wouldn't be seen if you were eyeballing the data in table form.

When you're examining a histogram, take note of each bar. The height of the bar represents how many values within a data set fall into a specific range. You're effectively using histograms to visualize grouping numeric values into ranges, which can be helpful when presenting test results, especially at a lower level of detail. Histograms can illustrate the distribution of values for your success or guardrail metrics in an A/B test.

Illustrating Test Analysis with Boxplots

Another technique to visualize your A/B test results is with a boxplot, also referred to as a box-and-whisker plot. You should use a boxplot if you'd like to present a better picture of your data analysis's distributional characteristics or would like to highlight outliers from test results. A boxplot can also display symmetry and skewness in the test data.

Let's circle back to the original For You A/B test from *Why You Should A/B Test*. In particular, the line graph on page 12 visualizes the increase in video plays when comparing the heavy consumption user subgroups from the test and control variants. See the following boxplot for a comparison of the same data, just displayed with the boxplot visual.

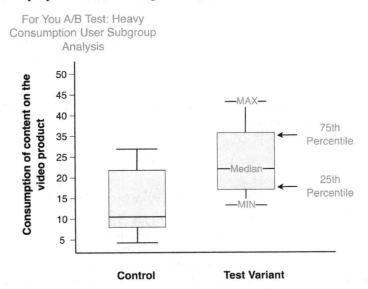

Let's dig into the anatomy of a boxplot. For users in the test variant that received the For You homepage, the following statistics were observed:

- Minimum video plays were 15.
- Maximum video plays were 45.
- Median video plays 25.

- The 25th percentile video plays 20.
- The 75th percentile video plays 35.

Take note of the degree of information presented in a boxplot compared to a line graph. The boxplot provides statistical data points that may be more helpful than a line graph, which lacks such information. The visual you select depends on your use case and the A/B test narrative you'd like to distill with your stakeholders.

Next, we'll explore how visuals can sometimes be misleading when summarizing A/B test results.

Presenting Misleading Results

One thing to note when visually representing A/B test results is the possibility of presenting misleading results. The following situations can lead to misleading results:

- Using a vertical scale (y-axis) that is too small or too big.

- Choosing a graph that looks presentable and maybe even more aesthetically pleasing but hides a clear interpretation by making things look smaller or larger.

- Cherry-picking the data by not including all the data in the graph and just the data that supports the objective or point the creator wants to get across.

In the next section, let's see what this looks like in practice with an example of a misleading graph. Make sure to check out the task in the sidebar, *Analyst Task: Identify How a Graph May Be Misleading*, beforehand to brainstorm on your own what makes the visualization misleading.

Analyst Task: Identify How a Graph May Be Misleading

Now that you have a general idea of how test results can be visually misleading, look at the graph on page 99. The goal of the visual is to present a narrative that suggests users in the holdback group for a cumulative holdback A/B test saw a dramatic increase in movie purchases on the CableMax video product during the evaluation period. In reality, the test results showed a mere .005 percent increase in purchases.

Brainstorm how this graph could give a false interruption of the demonstrated impact. We'll discuss this further in the following passage.

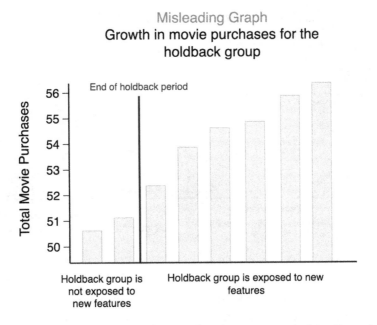

Misleading Graph
Growth in movie purchases for the holdback group

What did you observe when analyzing the data presented in the misleading graph? At first glance, movie purchases for the holdback group increased dramatically after exposure to the new features. However, if you zoom in, you'll notice the following:

- The y-axis does not start at zero.

- The y-axis scale is skewed to give the impression that there's a substantial increase in user growth, but rather, it's in the single digits.

- The x-axis is missing data to accurately showcase the purchase history during the holdback period. The magnitude looks impressive if you look at it from this scale, but what would it look like if the range for the x-axis included more data points during the holdback period?

Now look at the graph on page 100. The increase in movie purchases isn't as impressive when comparing this graph to the misleading graph. By extending the x-axis to include purchases for the entire span of the holdback period and evaluation period, the magnitude of movie purchases isn't quite as shocking.

This example illustrates how an interpretation of an A/B test is directly influenced by how the data is presented.

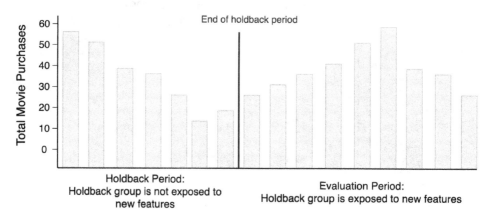

Now that you're familiar with data best practices, let's consider questions to keep in mind when creating visuals for your A/B test results in the sidebar *Chapter Roundup: Data Visualizations to Deliver A/B Test Results.*

Chapter Roundup: Data Visualizations to Deliver A/B Test Results

When running A/B tests on a product, you'll want the test results to speak for themselves. The less time you spend explaining the effect of a change, the more time you can spend brainstorming your next experiment. And the better your visualizations are, the easier the results are to interrupt. Ask yourself the following questions when assessing your data visualizations:

- Is the original nature of the data maintained in the visual?
- Is it easy to describe how the visual was constructed?
- Is it easy to mislead because of how the data distribution is summarized in the visual?

If you answered no to any of these questions, use two types of visualizations to present the results of an A/B test. For example, you could use both a histogram and a boxplot to summarize your A/B test results. Histograms, unlike boxplots, do keep the original nature of the data intact, making it an excellent graphic to accompany a boxplot.

Wrapping Up

Well done! You did a great job in navigating this data-intensive chapter. Soon enough, executives will be oohing and aahing over the huge metric gains so well illustrated by your data visualizations.

In this chapter, you learned to:

- Summarize A/B test results using visualizations like heatmaps and box-plots.

- Validate assumptions about a data set before querying, so you're not unknowingly misinterpreting specific fields.

- Calculate descriptive statistics to monitor for discrepancies and deviations in the data sets that power experimentation metrics.

- Observe visualizations for inaccurate and misleading information when interrupting the results of an A/B test.

- Correlate engineering system data with user data when validating A/B test outcomes.

Next, we'll dive into a key engineering decision. Should you build your A/B testing platform in-house or buy a third-party solution? What are the benefits of building versus buying? Answers to these questions are just a page turn away.

CHAPTER 5

To Build or to Buy an A/B Testing Platform

Imagine you're in your company's bi-weekly strategy meeting. A few minutes into the meeting, a colleague comes to you with a problem. They want to run experiments to evaluate product features but know that the engineering platform doesn't support A/B testing. You like innovating and solving problems, so you roll up your sleeves and dive headfirst to build a solution.

But, wait, does it *really* make sense to build an A/B testing platform from scratch? It's more than likely that someone else, whether it's an open source or a third-party vendor, has already solved this problem. Or you could build A/B testing logic on top of an existing engineering platform, such as the feature flag system. These are just some of the many factors to consider when deciding whether to build your A/B testing platform in-house or buy a third-party solution.

We know from the previous chapter that you need different types of data, such as user engagement data and metadata, to create your test results. We also know that leveraging data requires engineering investments to store, access, and query the data to understand the effect of changes in an A/B test. This chapter emphasizes the end-to-end system architecture, beyond your data infrastructure, that is needed to enable A/B testing on a product. Knowing what makes up an A/B testing platform will help you decide whether you should build the A/B testing platform in-house or integrate with a third-party solution. To be able to make that decision, we'll explore the following:

- Software architecture to facilitate A/B testing on a product.
- Engineering use cases that an A/B testing platform could support.
- Reasons to build a homegrown A/B testing platform or buy a third-party solution.

Like a cozy sweater that you return to when the seasons change, we'll return to our favorite company, CableMax, to demonstrate a basic implementation of an A/B testing platform. All right, let's do this!

Navigating the Classic Engineering Struggle

The age-old engineering dilemma is deciding to buy a vendor's product or build a system yourself. It's a tough decision, especially as more and more SaaS (software as a service) companies go to market.

In the case of A/B testing, a barrage of vendors is pushing experimentation solutions that promise to make your team more effective, efficient, and data-driven. Alternatively, there's *usually* a strong engineering desire to build a fancy new platform internally that will enable A/B testing on your product and ten other things at once. Regardless of which approach you select, be mindful of the most important problems you're solving as you decide.

Let's start by defining each approach. The first option, the homegrown solution, also called in-house, means that an engineering team within the company builds the platform to run experiments on the product. The second option, a third-party solution, also called the buy approach, entails integrating a platform or tool that fulfills most of the logic needed to enable A/B testing on a product.

Your approach depends on your current product engineering ecosystem and what matters to you. We'll discuss both in the following sections.

Assessing Your Current Engineering Landscape

To facilitate A/B testing on your product, you need data. No data means no A/B testing. The importance of data has been highlighted throughout the book, but to reiterate, here are reasons why you need data:

- To compute an experiment's metrics.
- To measure the performance of the engineering platform that your new product features are built on.

Knowing the need that data fulfills, are there regulatory policies that would prevent you from sharing your product and user data with an external system? Does your data consist of personally identifiable information, also referred to as PII, that should not be made available to third-party applications? If the answer to these questions is yes, building an in-house solution may be simpler than navigating the data policy requirements to use a third-party product.

Now let's assume you don't have any data restrictions dictating whether you should build an A/B testing platform in-house or buy a solution. Consider the following questions:

- Do you have engineers who are eager to architect and implement a new platform?

- Do you prefer access to the nitty-gritty details, like application logs or logs representing each step within the A/B testing process?

- Do you already have some key software components required of an A/B testing platform? Or would you have to build everything from scratch?

Asking these questions will start turning the gears to figure out what matters most to you. Integrating A/B testing into an engineering architecture that you didn't consider initially will be challenging whether you buy or build. You may have to start very simply with your A/B testing capabilities. Or you may, at some point, have to rebuild parts of your product if A/B testing was an afterthought.

Even with all these questions and details to consider, one thing is for sure: you don't need to build a vast engineering system before evaluating A/B testing as a concept. Let's start thinking about what is most important to you when enabling A/B testing on your product.

Defining What Matters to You

It's impossible to address every single variable that matters to your engineering and product teams when determining how to enable A/B testing on your product. To ease the decision process, think about the variables that are more critical than others.

Perhaps your main goal is to make it very simple and easy to run an experiment on the product. In that case, opting for the build solution is beneficial to customize it for your specific product.

Ask yourself questions to help determine what matters to you if it's unclear.

For instance, is your product in the hands of millions? If yes, your engineering platform scale should be critical in determining which approach to select.

Or does your organization already think there is unique value in evaluating changes with A/B testing? Or do you first need to prove the value of A/B testing? If the latter is the case, you may benefit from a third-party vendor solution that provides a small set of functionality to get the A/B testing gears moving quicker rather than later. Or you could build a very basic A/B testing platform in-house to showcase the value that A/B testing offers.

Knowing what variables are most important to you will help you decide how to tackle building the software and infrastructure to facilitate A/B testing on a product.

Next, let's dive into the basic design of an A/B testing platform so you know what to expect from your engineering systems.

Illustrating the Components of an A/B Testing Platform

You already know the anatomy of an A/B test and the various tests you can run on a product. Now it's time to connect all the dots and see what the engineering platform that enables A/B testing consists of. To decide whether an external A/B testing platform can provide the functionality needed to facilitate A/B testing on a product, it's best to know the high-level software components required of any experimentation platform.

In this section, we'll discuss the essential software requirements of an engineering system that orchestrates A/B testing, regardless of whether the system is a homegrown or a third-party solution. Your A/B testing solution should include every step of the experimentation process, from defining your test configuration and assigning users to variants to analyzing your test results.

First, let's look at your next task in the sidebar *Analyst Task: What Would You Expect from CableMax's A/B Testing Platform?*

Analyst Task: What Would You Expect from CableMax's A/B Testing Platform?

As promised, we're circling back to A/B testing at CableMax. What would you expect to see in an engineering system that facilitates A/B testing on CableMax's video product?

What software components are required to orchestrate A/B testing? For example, would you need a self-service tool to configure experiments?

Brainstorm a few ideas before we discuss further in the following section.

To illustrate an A/B testing platform, let's take a look at the homegrown solution built by the engineering team at CableMax. The platform consists of the following software components:

1. Variant Builder
2. Variant Assignment Web Service
3. Metrics Computation Pipelines
4. Self-Service A/B Test Configuration Tool

See the following image that illustrates the software components from the CableMax A/B testing platform.

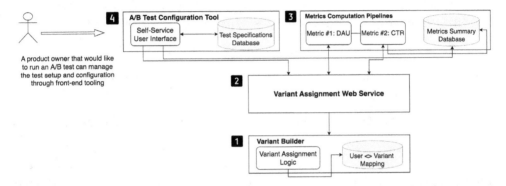

How does the CableMax architecture compare to what you initially brainstormed in the analyst task *Analyst Task: What Would You Expect from CableMax's A/B Testing Platform?* If you mapped a software component to each foundational piece of the A/B testing puzzle detailed in *Learn the Fundamentals of an A/B Test*, then you were spot on in defining the architecture. The first component, the Variant Builder, is responsible for the logic determining the user-to-variant mapping. This software contains the code that assigns users to the test and control variants. The second component, the Variant Assignment Web Service, gives access to the variants calculated by the builder component to front-end and server-side components that need to know when a user should be allocated into a new experience. The third component, the Metrics Computation Pipelines, computes a test's success and guardrail metrics for a test. The final piece, the Self-Service A/B Test Configuration Tool, enables your team to configure the definition of a test through a front-end application.

In the following section, let's explore each of these components in more detail.

Allocating Users to Test and Control Variants

The Variant Builder is the logic that decides which users are placed into an A/B test. More specifically, this software component is responsible for the following:

- Allocating users into the test and control variants; random assignment is necessary to ensure the test results are valid.

- Deallocating the users from the variants once the test is completed.

- Tagging users with an identifier that signifies to the system a clear mapping of a user to a variant.

- Ensuring there is no overlap; users should not be in multiple A/B tests that could conflict with each other and impact the test results.

You can take two approaches to assign users to variants:

- Batch allocation: randomly assign users to an experiment before the start date with an off-line batch process.

- Real-time allocation: randomly assign users to the test and control variants when they engage with the product in real time.

The batch allocation method randomly samples users to be placed in the control and test variants before the test starts. The primary benefit of batch allocation is the flexibility in determining the users you want to include in your variants. With a batch pipeline, you could easily use any data set to identify users to define the composition of your variants. For example, data scientists could execute complex queries to ensure enough users from varying demographics are well represented in the A/B test.

The downside to batch allocation is choosing users that fail to engage with the product for the particular weeks your test is running. You can't guarantee that the users will engage with the product during the duration of the test as they've been pre-identified before the test begins. Let's say your batch variant assignment selects users that are considered daily active users (DAU). In this case, it's not guaranteed that DAUs will use the product for the duration of the A/B test. For instance, maybe the users are on vacation or have deactivated their subscriptions after the variants were created.

The second method, by contrast, allocates users in real time to the test and control variants as they are exposed to a feature given the eligibility criteria. A key benefit of the real-time allocation approach is that new users can be incorporated into your experiment as soon as they subscribe to the product. The primary downside to this approach is the complexity it adds to your engineering logic that does the actual assignment.

You'll need to implement two steps to enable real-time allocation in the simplest form. First, fetch the A/B tests a user is currently assigned to. Second, validate whether the user should be included in the test based on the eligibility criteria. These two steps, when done in real time, could cause performance degradations. You should always keep performance in mind because it can affect how your users engage with the product. You wouldn't want a user to wait seconds, or worse, minutes, to load the user experience because the application checked if the user was allocated to an A/B test, right? For this reason, it never hurts to incorporate engineering system performance, such as time to load and latency, as guardrail metrics.

Whether you're using batch or real-time allocation to allocate users into a test, you'll need to ensure you've implemented a randomization algorithm to ensure the test results are valid. You'll also need to store the user-to-variant mappings to access for various use cases. To detail the use cases for the user to variant mappings further, look at the next analyst task in the sidebar *Analyst Task: What Would You Do with the User Variant Mappings* before we shift gears back to the A/B testing platform at CableMax.

Analyst Task: What Would You Do with the User Variant Mappings

Take a look at the high-level architecture diagram on page 107. What scenarios would benefit from the user variant mappings? In what contexts would you need to know which users have been assigned to a particular experiment's test or control variant?

Brainstorm ideas before we discuss further in the following passage.

Detailing the CableMax Variant Builder Database

Variant assignment methods aside, let's take a step back and visit the database that stores the user-to-variant mappings in the CableMax architecture. The image on page 110 represents the table schema from which the Variant Builder reads and writes to allocate users to a an experiment. The green table is populated by the self-service application when a product owner or engineer kicks off an A/B test. The Variant Builder populates the blue tables.

When you brainstormed scenarios requiring the user to variant mappings, did you consider the data analysis use case? It's common for data scientists to need access to the users within each variant to compute deeper data analysis beyond the success and guardrail metrics. Another scenario that requires the user-to-variant mappings is to identify the users already allocated to an ongoing A/B test so that you can avoid allocating a user into multiple tests simultaneously.

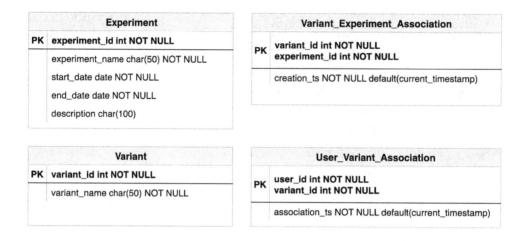

Whether you decide to build or buy your A/B testing platform, data scientists will want access to the user variant mappings for ad hoc analysis. To support this, you'll need to ensure your engineering platform makes the user variant associations easily accessible. This requirement leads us perfectly to the second software component in an A/B testing platform.

Accessing Variant Assignments

Now that you can calculate the users that get assigned to variants within an A/B test, let's reiterate scenarios that would require access to this data:

1. Product code that decides whether a user should receive feature A versus feature B based on the variant behavior and definition.

2. Data analysis to compute A/B test results; computing metrics for the test and control variants separately.

The front-end component to your product most likely will need access to the variant assignments. You could build the variant assignment logic into a library or web service. It really depends on your engineering design. The most critical factor is performance. Your users will feel a delay if accessing your A/B test variant assignments is slow.

Users expect the load time of the products they use to be in the low seconds, if not milliseconds. The perfect solution to prevent performance degradation would be to access the user to variant mappings locally, within the product application code, without any external web service calls or database connections. However, that's sometimes not feasible, especially for products that need to scale for millions of users.

Separating the access of the variants into a web service so that it can meet performance requirements may be your best approach for many reasons. First, a cache can be implemented to store the variant assignments for performance gains. This is an excellent idea if connecting to a database from a web service on the user request path is suboptimal. Second, the web service can be an abstraction layer in front of the datastore that includes additional enrichment to make sense of the user to variant mappings. For example, maybe the database stores just the user ID to the variant ID mapping, but you may need additional user metadata when accessing the variants from the application. In that case, the web service could look up the user metadata.

Defining the Metrics Computation Pipeline Component

In its simplest form, the Metrics Computation Pipeline processes data to derive insights for your A/B tests. You can have one data pipeline for each metric or consolidate the metrics that rely on similar data sets into the same pipeline. Remember that you'll need access to the variant assignments to calculate both the control and test variant metrics for each experiment. To really scale A/B testing in a product and engineering organization, the time it takes to get your test results should be minimal. Suppose it takes too long to get your hands on the experiment analysis. In that case, teams are less likely to adopt A/B testing to evaluate their product ideas.

For it to be possible to summarize test results and highlight key metrics, your product should already have basic instrumentation to create the events that will correlate to user engagement on the product, as mentioned in *Interface with Data and Visualizing Results*. The quality of the events that represent user actions on your product directly influences the metrics you can compute for your test results. For instance, if your product instrumentation is unreliably producing user click events, then the metrics that rely on clicks will be inaccurate. Remember to update your product's instrumentation as new features are built so that events are created to reflect the users interacting with the new feature.

Beyond computing metrics, an additional goal of your data pipelines is to get aggregate relevant data into a data warehouse or analytics tool for analysts to query from. When computing A/B results, keep in mind the complexities that come with using data. Make sure you monitor, prove your assumptions about the data, and ensure your test is statistically significant so your results are deemed valid.

Defining the A/B Testing Configuration Tool Component

What would you prefer, asking an engineer to kick off an A/B test or using a self-service application to configure the test yourself? For most, the answer is the latter. You want to be able to run tests as you wish, whenever you wish to do so.

The goal of a self-service tool is to simplify the process of creating and deploying an A/B test on the product. It should enable you to coordinate all the details necessary to kick off an A/B test. This tool is where you'll define the general specifications for your experiment, including the following:

- The guardrail and success metrics to measure the effectiveness of the test.
- The start and end of the test.
- The hypothesis of the test.
- The type of experiment selected.
- The eligibility criteria for the test and control variants.
- The owner of the test.

Sometimes things go differently than you expect when using A/B testing to evaluate changes in a product. In these instances, it'll be beneficial for this self-service A/B testing tool to include the ability to stop an A/B test at any moment, not just when the end date has arrived.

The easier the user interface is to set up and manage an experiment, the more likely you will increase the adoption of this experimentation methodology on a product. With this in mind, the tooling component shouldn't be an afterthought. The better your tooling is, the more likely you'll succeed in informing product decisions with A/B tests.

Now that you're familiar with the high-level software components needed to facilitate A/B testing on a product, let's explore whether to build or buy an A/B testing platform.

Building Versus Buying

By now, you've noticed a good amount of software is required to run an experiment on a product. Data infrastructure, tools to analyze the data, software to allocate users into variants, and an application are all needed to configure the A/B test.

The next question is how you will implement A/B testing on your product. Should you choose to build a solution in-house with your engineering team? Or should you integrate with a third-party product encapsulating most of the A/B testing logic?

Let's look at some of the benefits and drawbacks of both options so you can make the best decision possible.

Building a Homegrown A/B Testing Platform

The key to building a homegrown A/B testing platform is to start simple. The team that created the experimentation platform at Spotify initially started with a basic implementation that wrapped experiments around feature flags. There's no shame in building your A/B testing platform on top of existing concepts. As the product evolves and more experimentation capabilities are desired, your A/B testing platform will also evolve. Consider the following from the Spotify experimentation team:

Over time, interest in A/B testing grew, and in 2013 we decided to spin up a team to take on building a more robust system. Thus was born ABBA, an A/B testing system that allowed us to (more) easily run experiments. Now we had a place to see what A/B tests were actually running and a pipeline that computed results. The introduction of the system was a step change in productivity, and over time it was integrated into pretty much every aspect of Spotify—in our desktop clients and mobile clients, web services and data pipelines, in-app messaging, and email campaigns.[1]

It can be overwhelming, especially if there's a sense of urgency in which folks ask questions like, "Why can't we run A/B tests on the product today?" In cases like this, take a phased approach to build an in-house solution. Start by picking the most critical pieces to build first. For example, you don't need sophisticated allocation logic for variant assignments; instead, implement a simple batch process that randomly samples users to start.

Similarly, it's worth emphasizing that a lot can be accomplished with very little. You can start with a small engineering team. If the team consists of three engineers, then describe the engineering system's requirements. For example, rather than building fancy tools to determine the demographics or dimensions to create subgroups, you can manually run ad hoc queries to get this data. Start small, then build your way up.

Let's brainstorm how the CableMax A/B testing platform architecture could be simplified in the next task in the sidebar *Analyst Task: How Would You Simplify CableMax Architecture?* on page 114.

---

1.   https://engineering.atspotify.com/2020/10/spotifys-new-experimentation-platform-part-1/

Analyst Task: How Would You Simplify CableMax Architecture?

Take a look at the high-level architecture diagram on page 107. What changes to the general implementation could you make to the homegrown A/B testing platform that would simplify the architecture?

Brainstorm ideas before we discuss further in the following passage.

The CableMax team wants to simplify the architecture for the A/B testing platform that was built in-house. A few shortcuts could be made to the homegrown solution on page 107 to reduce complexity. The team may lack data engineering skills to maintain the data pipelines responsible for daily metric computation. If that's the case, you could perform manual data analysis using notebooks instead of building an automated metrics pipeline illustrated by the Metrics Computation Pipelines component.

Another idea is to directly engage with the engineering team to manually set up the A/B test instead of investing engineering time to implement a self-service user interface. In this case, asking the engineering team may feel like a bottleneck, which initially is OK. It's better to start gaining user insights and collecting data by running A/B tests to evaluate product ideas than to wait for the perfect A/B testing platform.

Next, let's explore the benefits of building a homegrown solution to A/B testing.

Highlighting the Advantages of the Build Approach

Consider the following advantages of building a homegrown A/B testing solution:

- Expertise in the software resides within your team. If the software has a defect, you could easily reach out to the engineering team that built it. However, suppose you've purchased a third-party solution. In that case, the expertise to debug any issues that may arise may not exist at your company but instead requires a consultant from the third-party vendor.

- Data to compute test results or assign users to variants is contained within your engineering ecosystem, even the sensitive or PII data.

- Logic tightly coupled to your product code and deployment architecture should create the ideal developer experience over time.

- Customization will be easier because an internal engineering team will be dedicated to evolving the capabilities over time.

- Ownership of the end-to-end solution will allow you to scale on your own timeline.

Sometimes it's best to learn from others, especially when they've vetted both approaches. Check out the article "A/B Testing Framework: Build or Buy?" on Redfin's engineering blog for insights into their experiences evaluating the buy versus build approaches. In particular, take note of the reason for choosing to build the A/B testing platform in-house:

From our experience using a third party, we had gained a deep appreciation for the ability to dig into the raw data to debug surprising results. We were more convinced we wanted the ability to connect our A/B results with internal business metrics. 90% of the companies we talked with had built their own and were happy with their choice.[2]

We've discussed the benefits of building an in-house A/B testing platform. Next, we'll highlight the drawbacks.

Highlighting the Disadvantages of the Build Approach

Now that you're familiar with the advantages of a homegrown approach, let's dive into the bad. The disadvantages are the following:

- Time it may take to develop a platform from the ground up. Building an A/B testing platform entirely from scratch is time-consuming and requires deep product integration. You can create a minimal implementation quickly, but you'll undoubtedly need to spend time improving the usability and durability of the system later on.

- Requirements for diverse skill sets within your engineering teams to build an end-to-end platform. For example, you'll need front-end engineers to create the self-service tooling, back-end engineers to implement the web service, and data engineers to develop the metrics pipelines.

- Cost in terms of time, engineering effort, and infrastructure spend can easily be underestimated. In comparison, it's easy to gauge the cost of your third-party software every month.

To combat the time-to-build concern, open source libraries and tools can help you hit the ground running as you evolve your in-house solution over time. If you go this route, the activity on the project's GitHub repository is worth noting as you select your open source solutions. If the Github repository

---

2.   https://www.redfin.com/news/a-b-testing-build-or-buy/

suggests it hasn't been updated in a year, then the support for the tool may be minimal. Or, if a tool has little documentation, it may be harder to integrate.

Now you know the good and bad of building a homegrown solution to A/B test changes on your product. Next, let's focus on the reasoning behind building an A/B testing platform from a third-party solution.

Integrating with a Third-Party Solution

When you hear the word "buy," translate that to integration with a third-party service or external platform. If you're curious about what products are available, enter "A/B testing software vendors" as your search criteria on google.com. The search results may be overwhelming; many vendors are building similar A/B testing solutions.

Before we detail the benefits and drawbacks, let's first talk about the financial cost. The cost you'll pay is usually incurred on the scale in which you leverage the third-party product and the support from the vendor to consult your team during integration or triaging issues. Sometimes the amount you pay is determined by how many users you incorporate into your experiments. The more users you have on your product, the more it may cost you to run A/B tests through a third-party solution.

Let's explore the advantages of integrating with an external platform to move forward with A/B testing on your product.

Highlighting the Advantages of the Third-Party Approach

Depending on your engineering team's situation, you may not be ready to invest time and energy toward building an internal platform. Opting for an external solution to incorporate A/B testing into your product may make sense. The advantages of choosing a third-party solution to enable A/B testing on your product include the following:

- Time to production may be reduced compared to building the platform internally. It's hard to say this for sure, as integration with the third-party application varies and still requires time and effort from your engineering team. Be mindful of the lift an integration takes and how that compares with the internal approach.

- Infrastructure may be supported by the third-party vendor, translating to less software overall to manage by your engineering team.

Let's elaborate on how opting for the buy approach will speed up your time to start A/B testing. Organizationally, is your engineering team small? And does your product team want to move quickly to start A/B testing as soon as possible? If that's the case, sometimes the third-party approach can get you further faster by off-loading a lot of the front-end development and data-intensive computation logic to the third-party tooling. However, if you decide to off-load complex statistical computations, make sure you trust the logic under the hood. You need to trust the logic provided by the third-party A/B testing platform; otherwise, your product team will be less likely to make decisions on how to evolve the product based on A/B test results.

Highlighting the Disadvantages of the Third-Party Approach

The disadvantages of integrating with an external platform to facilitate the A/B testing logic on your product include the following:

- Variable subscription costs for the A/B testing functionality and support services. Depending on the scale of your product, the price can build up and become quite expensive. The more tests your run, the more expensive it may be.

- Limited customization and integration functionality with your product codebase.

- Key company data may need to be exposed to the third-party application to compute metrics and assign users to variants. There may be restrictions on the data you can share with an external platform.

- Difficulty debugging issues when the expertise of the system that contains the essential logic for an A/B test is outside your engineering team.

- Narrow metrics-reporting capabilities that could make it more difficult to understand the effect of an experiment on your product and business metrics. The metrics that come out of the box with an external platform may be too general or not specific enough for your product needs.

If you buy an A/B testing platform solution, keep in mind the work involved with integrating your product with the vendor's application. How easy would it be to extend your user engagement data sets to a third-party system? If it's complex or cumbersome, this may be a reason to build in-house. It won't be as simple as "enable this A/B testing feature for everyone," so when evaluating, ensure you understand the core architecture and integration logistics.

It's also worth considering the impact on your engineering system metrics if you select a third-party solution. Adding an external library or interfacing with services owned by the third-party vendor may increase the time to load when a user engages with features on your product. If the performance of your product degrades, it could impact key business and product metrics and inadvertently negatively influence your A/B test results.

Next, we'll detail other use cases your A/B testing platform may serve, which could influence your decision to buy or build.

Extending the Scope of an A/B Testing Platform

It's worth highlighting that the software that supports A/B testing can also aid many other use cases. The use cases that go beyond experimentation include the following:

- Feature flags
- User cohorts
- Data analysis
- Targeting campaigns

We'll quickly detail how these use cases are enabled by very similar logic that's in place in a typical A/B testing platform. You might be wondering why we're discussing these additional features. You're more likely to invest in the design of an engineering platform if there are multiple use cases it can support. Alternatively, if your peers or key executives are pushing back on building A/B testing capabilities within the product, consider leaning into these other capabilities to highlight the many benefits of A/B testing. We'll discuss more strategies for advocating for A/B testing within an organization that's less than supportive in *Cultivate a Test-Friendly Culture.*

Deploying with Feature Flags

A feature flag is a mechanism to release a software change to production to enable or disable the new feature to users. Another term for enabling or disabling a new feature in the context of feature flags is gating or ungating. Suppose you decide to ungate, or enable, a new feature deployed to production to a subset of users. In that case, you could leverage the user tagging component in an A/B testing engineering system to create the group of users for which the feature is ungated.

A feature flag controls the availability of a code or design change to a product's user base. In practice, a feature flag is used to roll out a change to users, sometimes incrementally or after it's been vetted in an A/B test. The similarity between feature flags and A/B testing is that both require a component that assigns users to a specific group and exposes them to a new feature. This similarity is often why A/B testing platforms encapsulate feature flag functionality. Alternatively, sometimes feature flag tooling evolves into an A/B testing platform.

For more on feature flags, read this interesting article on Uber's engineering blog titled, "Introducing Piranha: An Open Source Tool to Automatically Delete Stale Code."[3] The article details an open source solution to address the downside to utilizing feature flags in your code: identifying those feature flags that are deprecated, rolled back, or have been live in production for a good amount of time that would suggest the flag itself is obsolete. The article is also a good introduction to using feature flags in a production setting.

Digging Deeper with User Cohorts

No rule suggests you can't leverage the user assignments crafted for A/B test variants outside the scope of the test itself. With deeper-cut user cohort definitions, you create a practice within your product engineering teams to understand how specific user groups engage with your product with general data analysis. For instance, you could leverage more granular user cohorts to answer the following questions:

- Which demographic of users has the lowest number of DAUs?
- Which age group prefers not to engage with a specific feature or area of the product?

You'll never regret your time spent understanding how specific user groups engage or interact with your product. This is similar to how you'll never regret improving your data ecosystem, as you'll see in the next section.

Expanding Data Set Usage

The data sets used to compute metrics could extend to additional use cases beyond A/B testing, such as the following:

- Ad hoc analysis conducted by data scientists and analysts.
- Features to train machine learning models.
- Product metrics tracked week over week outside the scope of an experiment.

When you have easily accessible data, people want to use it to power their decisions or enable the product features they're building.

---

3.   https://eng.uber.com/piranha/

Supporting Targeting Capabilities

Targeting is a close neighbor to A/B testing. Targeting campaigns are leveraged most often within the advertising and marketing sectors of a company, but they can extend to general product and business use cases in which there's a desire to increase the reach of content to a particular user group. For example, teams can utilize targeting for the following use cases:

- Reach users that are more likely to engage with a particular promotion or feature.

- Combat banner blindness, when users consciously or unconsciously ignore banner-like content if they're personalized toward their usage and engagement habits.

- Distribute pricing variations to specific user groups that are more likely to increase profits or engage with the advertisement that pushes the pricing change.

- Offer different tiers of services to select groups that prior research suggests would benefit most.

To illustrate the synergies between the targeting use case and A/B testing, take a look at the following analyst task in the sidebar *Analyst Task: Promoting a New TV Show on the For You Homepage.*

Analyst Task: Promoting a New TV Show on the For You Homepage

The For You A/B test increased the usage of personalization features at CableMax. The goal was to create an experience that users could trust to find their favorite movies and TV shows and discover new content recommended just for them.

Given the success, the marketing team has their eye on using the For You homepage for their content promotion needs. They would like to promote a new TV show by targeting users through the homepage. This promotion would be presented as a large banner at the top of the page—prime real estate.

However, the promotion may be presented to users who dislike the TV show. If this happens, it could be a jarring experience as the content feels less personal to the user's taste. Ideally, you want to maintain the user's trust in the For You homepage. To address this concern, the marketing team will promote the new TV show to specific user cohorts likely to engage with it, given their prediction logic.

How does A/B testing play a role in validating this targeting campaign? Think about this question before we discuss it further in the following passage.

The beauty of A/B testing is that you can use it to understand the impact of targeting initiatives. In the CableMax use case detailed in the most recent task, the marketing team explores using the For You homepage to promote content. The marketing team's goal is to target users who they've predicted to have an affinity for a new TV show by surfacing a promotional row at the top of the For You homepage. See the image that follows.

PROMO: New TV Show

Check out this new show!

Movies For You

Continue Watching Your Shows

When brainstorming how to use A/B testing to ensure the CableMax marketing targeting efforts are effective, did you consider separating a portion of the targeted user group into a control group? If so, that's a great idea because it would enable answers to the following questions:

- Did users in the targeted group who were predicted to watch the new TV show watch more episodes compared to similar users, the control group, who didn't receive the promotion on their homepage?

- Did users in the targeted group discover the new TV show through the promotion on their For You homepage?

- Did users in the targeted group see a decrease in engagement because it no longer felt personalized because of the promotional targeting campaign at the top of the page?

Targeting Campaign

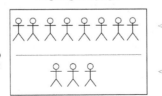

Effectiveness of the targeting campaign can be measured by comparing engagement of the two subgroups, similar to that of a test and control variant in A/B testing.

Promotional row is presented to the majority of the users in the targeted user group.

A **small subset** of the targeted user group will not receive the promotional row, serving as a control group.

Business and marketing teams typically do not want a large portion of their targeted audience partitioned into a control group because that decreases the exposure of their promotional efforts. When using A/B testing to measure the effectiveness of a targeting campaign, be wary of this by taking a conservative approach to determining the sample size of your control group.

If you're undecided about whether to buy or build, reflect on what matters most to you when building an engineering platform. Check out *Chapter Roundup: What Factors Matter Most to You?* for variables that may influence your decision.

Chapter Roundup: What Factors Matter Most to You?

Both strategies have merits, whether you're building an engineering platform internally or integrating with a third-party tool. Making this decision depends on your organization's needs and requirements.

Consider the following questions to determine what factors matter most to you when deciding on how to build an A/B testing platform.

- Versatility: can you easily adapt or make changes to your A/B testing logic when needed? If this is important, then the homegrown solution is ideal.

- Performance: does latency matter if the user allocation is done in real time? Can your engineering systems handle the additional A/B testing logic to shift traffic for a subset of users to a new feature?

- Timing: what is the risk of starting later when comparing the time it would take to build versus buying? Starting simple with a homegrown solution may be ideal unless integration with a third-party service is minimal and seamless.

- Trust: which solution would increase trust and reduce fear of failing or mistakes happening? When introducing a process change to the product development life cycle, you want people to trust the underlying logic and results produced from the experiment. The more trust they have using the A/B testing platform that informs decisions made on the product, the better.

- Extensibility: do you want to get more out of your A/B testing engineering system? Would you like to implement targeting capabilities that run alongside or within the software components that facilitate A/B testing?

While thinking about these questions, think about what matters most to you and use that to lead you to the ideal A/B testing solution for your product.

Wrapping Up

Great job! You've navigated all the details concerning buying or building your A/B testing platform! It's an important decision that influences how A/B testing is facilitated on your product.

Here's what we covered in this chapter:

- The software components, such as a self-service application and logic to assign users to a variant, that are needed within an engineering system to orchestrate A/B testing.

- The advantages and disadvantages of integrating with a third-party application and a homegrown solution to facilitate the experimentation logic on your product.

- The use cases, such as feature flags and user targeting, that an A/B testing system could extend to support.

Now that you're well prepared to decide whether to build or buy your A/B testing platform, you're likely exuding excitement. You're ready to run lots of A/B tests on your product.

Well, hold tight for a second there.

Not everyone you work with may share such a perspective. You may find yourself in an organization that needs to be convinced of the benefits. If this is the case, you'll need some assistance cultivating an experimentation-driven culture. The next chapter will explore tactics and strategies to advocate for an experimentation-driven culture within your product engineering organization. With these methods, you'll ease the transition to running A/B tests on your product like a pro in no time!

CHAPTER 6

Cultivate a Test-Friendly Culture

We saved the best for last—the human aspect of introducing A/B testing as a step in product development. Technology is complex, but humans are far more complex. When building an engineering platform, what motivates, incentivizes, and drives individuals are often of little concern. But they should be top of mind when cultivating a culture that embraces experimentation. Motivating teams to use A/B testing to ensure changes are monitored for impact is contingent on your team's culture.

In the previous chapter, we focused on the advantages and disadvantages of building an engineering platform in-house versus integrating with a third-party vendor's solution. If you're in an opinion-driven culture or on a team where A/B testing has yet to be adopted, the process and engineering platform directly influences your A/B testing practices. With a trusted and seamless process, you're more likely to increase adoption of the A/B testing methodology among your peers and teams.

In this chapter, we'll focus on the following:

- Tactics to create a culture of experimentation.
- Reasons why A/B testing may not be embraced or welcomed.
- Strategies to increase the adoption of A/B testing.

If you're unsure if your team culture will embrace A/B testing, consider this question: is your team more interested in being correct or more interested in demonstrating whether their ideas have the impact they expect? If it's the former, then let's take steps toward creating an ideal culture in which A/B testing is embraced to the full extent! If it's the latter, consider this chapter your guide to easing the transition to incorporating A/B testing in your product development life cycle.

Breaking Down the Resistance

Shifting from a culture where the loudest voice in the room decides how the product evolves, whether you're at a small or big company, is a challenging feat. Valuing the user and product insights gained from experiments over the decision to launch a feature will take time. You'll need to be patient and strategic as you shift how features are added to your product. Before we explore tactics to increase the adoption of A/B testing, let's consider why this experimentation methodology can be met with resistance.

Identifying Why A/B Testing May Not Be Embraced

The common reasons for not adopting A/B testing within a product engineering organization include the following:

- Fear of being wrong. You may have an intuition, and without A/B testing, you could push the change straight to production. Nothing is in your way from seeing your change in the hands of your users, not even data that would suggest the feature could be better.

- Lack of trust in the data or the A/B testing engineering platform. The platform may have a history of producing inclusive results from misconfigured tests. Or the data pipelines that compute key metrics often fail or are delayed by weeks.

- Desire for quick cycles to production, avoiding the extra steps needed to run and evaluate an experiment.

Now that we know why A/B testing could be met with resistance, let's return to A/B testing at CableMax for an example of a company that initially did not embrace A/B testing.

Creating a Culture of Experimentation at CableMax

Let's go back to before the For You homepage A/B test was launched and imagine what it was like to introduce a new feature on the CableMax video product. The A/B testing platform didn't exist. The product team was accustomed to designing and immediately launching product features directly requested by the executive leadership team without an evaluation step. .

The product development life cycle looked similar, if not identical, to the figure on page 127.

As a data-driven analyst, you were accustomed to vetting changes with A/B testing and using the data to influence product decisions. Before A/B testing,

the executive leadership team highly influenced the product roadmap. It started with an email sent by the VP of Product to suggest a new feature was urgent and should be built ASAP. Next, the team scrambled to implement it. Then once implemented, the feature was shipped to production for all users to engage with. Since the A/B testing step was skipped, it was unclear how the feature influenced product, business, and user metrics.

For most teams, this way of working was acceptable. They were used to not knowing how their changes affected essential metrics. However, as a critical member of the personalization team, you knew that you could do better. Once the idea of the For You homepage came about, you advocated for the team to build an A/B testing platform to evaluate not just the new homepage but also any new features in the future.

Fast forward to when the A/B testing platform was ready for use! You assumed teams would be eager to evaluate their grand product features using the platform. Unfortunately, this wasn't the case. Your product and engineering partner teams weren't as enthusiastic as you were about leveraging this experimentation methodology on the product.

Before we dive deeper, let's pause for a second to look at your first analyst task for this chapter in the sidebar *Analyst Task: Why Do You Think A/B Testing Was Not Initially Embraced at CableMax?*

Analyst Task: Why Do You Think A/B Testing Was Not Initially Embraced at CableMax?

Why do you think product teams were wary of using the A/B testing at CableMax? Brainstorm this before we discuss it further in the following section.

At CableMax, once the A/B testing was built, nobody trusted the engineering that facilitated the logic on the product. Concerns were that the right users were not allocated to the test and control variants. Similarly, there was minimal trust in the data used to compute the test results. Because user engagement and product metrics weren't monitored to the granularity needed in an A/B test, there was no reason prior for having a scalable data engineering platform.

What reasons for resistance to A/B testing did you brainstorm in the most recent analyst task? If you thought the product team was reluctant that their ideas might not flesh out as they expected, then you're spot on. Incorporating A/B testing is a process change that impacts not only the product development timeline but also impacts which changes make it into the hands of users. The product team had to shift their success metrics from the number of new features shipped to production to the impact and effectiveness of those features. Imagine how big of a change this is to how a product team works. Once A/B testing is embraced, it doesn't only change product decisions and outcomes but also what you talk about in your meetings. Meetings no longer focus on the number of features launched but on what specific features influenced metrics.

If you're advocating for an experimentation-driven culture at your job, the struggle to accept A/B testing at CableMax may be too familiar. Shifting the way of working is tricky but doable. To pivot your team's perspective, emphasize the benefits of A/B testing and how it can combat their hesitancies to embrace it.

Shifting Your Team's Perspective

Once you know why your team is resistant to A/B testing, you can then focus your energy on framing the benefits and process so it addresses their concerns. Let's look at how to manage a few common reasons teams are not implementing A/B tests on their product.

Prototyping for Quicker Iterations and Insights

Let's say your team is worried about the extra time it takes to evaluate product ideas. Is it quicker to ship your code straight from development to production for all your users to engage with? Yes, definitely. However, there are ways you can combat this concern.

If this is the case, lean into building prototypes. Aim to build a minimal version of the new feature or change, and A/B test that to avoid over-engineering or spending too much time on an idea before it's been adequately evaluated with an A/B test. Once you gain insights from your A/B test, you can decide on one of two options:

1. Proceed with the change by polishing the original minimal implementation and evaluating the latest version, which would be a launch candidate.

2. Keep the user and product insights but throw out the idea because it didn't move metrics or perform as expected.

See the following image that shows the product release timeline emphasizing prototyping for quicker insights.

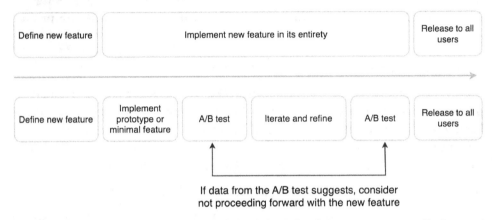

If data from the A/B test suggests, consider not proceeding forward with the new feature

With the prototyping approach illustrated in the figure, you typically have at least two iterations to collect data. Time and energy are finite, and you want to ensure you're spending time on the right work that can have the impact you most desire, whether on the user experience or critical business metrics.

If a feature is evaluated but not launched to all users, it shouldn't be considered a loss because you did learn something new about your product and the users who engage with it. The earlier you realize a change will not result in the desired impact, the earlier your engineering and product teams can refocus their efforts on ideas that could be more promising.

By A/B testing ideas and changes made to a product, you gain user and product insights into how changes influence or affect metrics. If you're not gaining insights, you're likely spending months on projects or new features that may not move your metrics in the right direction or, worse, move in the negative direction.

Informing Product Strategy

Another way to frame the need for A/B testing for your product and engineering organization is to emphasize that with the right metrics, the data from your experiments will complement your product strategy. If your product strategy is correct in meeting your users' needs and influencing key metrics, consider A/B testing as a means to provide feedback that you're moving in the right direction.

A/B testing is a feedback loop that either supports the vision your product and engineering leads have created or influences a pivot or alternative strategy. Perhaps the data from your A/B test results identify new opportunities that you otherwise wouldn't know if you didn't use this experimentation methodology to evaluate ideas on a subset of users. Either way, using A/B tests to evaluate iterations to your product will help inform your product strategy.

Making the A/B Testing Process Seamless

Another common reason for resisting A/B testing is a lack of trust in the process. Trust and ease of use are related. If something is convoluted and hard to use, teams will be less likely to trust it. Teams are more likely to trust the outcome and results if something is straightforward to use. Investing in the A/B testing process to increase adoption is well worth it.

Attributes of a seamless A/B testing process include the following:

- The platform is reliable, consistently producing results for each experiment.

- The process of setting up the test isn't too burdensome. Make the process so convenient that your teammates and peers have no reason not to use it.

- The experiment can be set up by anyone.

If you're just starting with A/B testing, it will take time to build a frictionless process. The ultimate goal is for anyone and everyone that works at your company to be able to run an A/B test. The more people that can run A/B tests on your product, the more you'll increase the adoption of the methodology. You wouldn't want to gatekeep or prevent teams from running A/B tests; it's a methodology meant for anyone who wants to understand the effect of their changes on a product.

Your process should also include a forum for educating teams on the results of past experiments. Beyond the team that set up an A/B test, other teams will benefit from understanding an experiment's configuration and learning from the test results. To enable such, you could create a post-test analysis review meeting that meets bi-weekly to do the following:

- Examine the test results.

- Identify areas for improvement in the process that would influence the roadmap for the team that built the A/B testing platform.

- Discuss whether to launch the feature or revisit the solution implemented.

This open forum will provide transparency for other teams to easily learn and encourage a culture of welcoming surprising outcomes. It will also naturally lead to discussions to improve the A/B testing process, such as improving how to set up a test or updating metric definitions. The post-test analysis review meeting serves as a feedback loop for the team that supports the A/B testing platform. The overarching goal of this meeting should be to emphasize user and product insights gained so it sparks curiosity for other teams to gain similar insights.

The more accessible and trustworthy the A/B testing process is, the easier it'll be to create demand.

Focusing on Gaining Product Insights

Simple statements can sometimes be profound. For example, if you're learning more about your product and how users engage with the product, you're winning. Suppose you're shipping changes to production without any awareness of the effect of that change on critical metrics. In that case, you're not learning more about your user's engagement habits and not winning.

Similarly, simple questions can also be profound. For instance, consider these questions:

- What was your team's impact on key business metrics?
- What was the impact of your work from the past quarter or year?
- What should you build next quarter?

When you start A/B testing, you may realize that a large percentage of changes or new features have little to no effect on your metrics. The decisions and ideas you thought were a slam dunk were no more than an inelegant belly-flop into the shallow end of a swimming pool. You're exchanging your old problems for new problems. Your new problem will be to improve your product understanding by allowing A/B testing to help you identify areas worth investing in with the highest payback. Maybe minor improvements like the color or spacing of your design components will result in significant metric gains. Perhaps more extensive changes to your machine learning algorithms will trigger more significant gains. With A/B testing, you have data insights to make better decisions rather than relying on your feelings or intuition.

Before A/B testing, changes are launched to users without measuring the effect or influence on business and product metrics. So technically, there's little to no fear of being wrong with your new feature ideas. You may measure the success of a product and engineering team on the number of features delivered. However, after A/B testing, the measure of success should be on the impact on your key product and business metrics. This shift is what causes many organizations to not embrace A/B testing.

In an article titled "Building a Culture of Experimentation," Stefan Thomke details the culture at Booking.com that was in part built by the Director of Experimentation, Lukas Vermeer. At Booking.com, a culture of curiosity was fostered by enabling anyone (product owners, designers, developers, or writers) to run an A/B test as they wish. Specifically, this sentiment is expressed in the following statement:

In experimental cultures, employees are undaunted by the possibility of failure. "The people who thrive here are curious, open-minded, eager to learn and figure things out, and OK with being proven wrong," said Vermeer, who now oversees all testing at Booking.com. The firm's recruiters look for such people, and to make sure they're empowered to follow their instincts, the company puts new hires through a rigorous onboarding process, which includes experimentation training, and then gives them access to all testing tools.[1]

If you focus on the impact you're creating and the insights you're gaining, you'll relinquish any fears of evaluating ideas that may not work out as expected. The data to support the insights about your product are more valuable than your intuition being correct.

With A/B testing, your team gains a sense of freedom. Freedom to try any idea, freedom to build multiple versions and evaluate which version is best for your users. With this freedom, innovation can happen. Your ideas become bolder, and your team's appetite to experiment increases.

A test-friendly culture will elevate apprehensions around decision-making. When there's less emphasis on getting a design or feature right the first time, there are fewer debates on the ideal solution the engineering or design team should build because multiple solutions can easily be evaluated. Your team will have less fear of getting it wrong and an increased focus on trying out ideas and learning from them. This sentiment is empowering—to see any idea tested and potentially launched if the data suggests doing so is what great products and great companies are made from.

Next, let's explore how to incorporate A/B testing into an organization that's not using this methodology as part of the product development life cycle.

---

1.   https://hbr.org/2020/03/building-a-culture-of-experimentation

Rolling Out A/B Testing Within Your Organization

Change is hard.

Change is especially hard when altering how we work and the culture we're most familiar with. Creating and executing a product vision is more straightforward than spending additional time and energy measuring the improvement. Finding the right metrics or exploring alternative solutions can be challenging if your original idea doesn't have the desired impact. Measuring the effect of your product changes on user engagement introduces the potential to be wrong about the vision and the features you're building.

Most organizations that do not A/B test consider simply shipping a new feature as a success regardless of the impact that feature had on key business and product metrics. With A/B testing, you add a step before a product and engineering team can declare a change successful. The key to rolling out this type of change within a product organization is to do the following:

- Standardize the process so it's easy to adopt.

- Form a small group of experts who can help answer questions and provide support.

- Gain support from leaders at the top.

- Lean into market research supporting the change.

- Understand what motivates your peers and teammates so you can make small changes to serve their needs better.

Now we'll dive into the specifics to support each tactic.

Standardizing the Creation of A/B Tests

If your goal is to increase adoption, first focus on standardizing the process to create and launch an A/B test. The main benefits here are to ensure everyone follows the same guidelines and identify areas in which tooling could make it easier to facilitate A/B testing.

To standardize the process of A/B testing, create a template that defines the essential details needed to launch a test. The testing template would include the following:

1. Experiment name: a unique identifier to reference your test by.

2. Experiment description: a brief description for other teams to understand what is being tested.

3. Hypothesis statement: your belief or prediction that you aim to demonstrate with data.

4. Success and guardrail metrics: the metrics you'll use to monitor performance that will also influence if the feature or change should launch to all your users.

5. Eligibility criteria: qualification criteria for a user to be included in the variants.

6. Start and end date: when you expect to start and end the test.

7. Team contact information: the teams accountable for the test experience.

Luckily you're already familiar with the concepts in the testing template, as it's the anatomy of an A/B test detailed in *Learn the Fundamentals of an A/B Test*.

With a standardized A/B test template, you're reducing the barrier of entry for anyone to run an A/B test on the product. What is needed to facilitate A/B testing on your product shouldn't be a mystery. A template clarifies what's expected to run a test and continues with one of the key themes to cultivating a test-friendly culture: the democratization of A/B testing.

Once you've created your template, you can identify areas that teams struggle to fill out. For example, if teams are unsure what metrics to select, you could create a metrics guide with example use cases. Or you may find that teams need help writing a clear hypothesis statement. If so, consider writing a step-by-step experimentation guide that includes the semantics of the hypothesis statement.

The document that serves as the test configuration template should be reviewed by folks familiar with A/B testing best practices. The review process should reduce the number of misconfigured tests launched to production. The more experienced teams get at running experiments, the more efficient they'll be at configuring them. Before that's the case, having a method for hand-holding those unfamiliar with A/B testing specifications would be helpful. Now you may be asking who should review each test or how it should be reviewed. This can be done by a handful of individuals that compose an experimentation review committee, which you'll explore next.

Creating an Experimentation Review Committee

Once the A/B testing floodgates are open, anyone at your company should be able to run an experiment. In this case, you'll want to add guardrails to prevent misconfigured tests from making their way into production.

You can't guarantee issues will not arise at some point, especially as you increase the number of simultaneous tests running on the product. However, you can catch test configuration issues earlier rather than later, in particular before the experiment is active, by creating an experimentation review committee.

The experimentation review committee is a small, cross-functional group of individuals. The goals of the committee are the following:

- Inspect test configurations by checking that the fundamental components are accurate. Does the test have a well-defined hypothesis? Is the sample size correct? Should there be guardrail metrics?

- Support teams by answering questions such as aborting tests early if the metrics suggest a large degradation or including new users in their variants to combat novelty effects.

- Promote A/B testing by sharing results from past tests and advocating for those who have an interest but don't have the time to set up an experiment.

When establishing the committee, define the goals for the group and measure progress toward those goals. If your main goal is to promote A/B testing so it's further adopted into your team's product development life cycle, then you could keep track of the user and product insights gained from each A/B test. Other metrics that are worth monitoring to support the experimentation review committee include the following:

- Number of tests reviewed.
- Number of successful tests.
- Number of misconfigured tests.

Over time, the number of misconfigured tests should decrease as the experimentation committee improves the review process. Similarly, successful tests should increase as teams learn how to properly set up tests with help from the experimentation committee. The more tests that produce trustworthy results, the more likely teams will add this evaluation step to their product development process.

Circling back to A/B testing at CableMax, the experimentation review committee consisted of the following:

- Representative from the business team to ensure business metrics were always top of mind, or at least a guardrail metric.

- Product managers to confirm that the correct product features are scheduled and coordinated.

- Engineers to ensure a test wouldn't break the platform or engineering logic.

- Data scientists to review test configurations to ensure validity in the test results.

Including a representative from the business team was a strategic decision. At CableMax, the business team influences how the product evolves. This may not be the case at other companies, so it wouldn't be necessary to include them in the committee.

Before continuing, let's look at your next task in the sidebar *Analyst Task: What Are the Benefits of a Review Committee?*

Analyst Task: What Are the Benefits of a Review Committee?

Keeping in mind the reasons for the resistance to adopting A/B testing into the product development cycle, what do you think are the major benefits of an experimentation review committee? Brainstorm this before we discuss the benefits in the following passage.

If you're questioning why it's necessary to review A/B test specifications, think about the impact of a misconfigured test launched to production. A misconfigured test could delay the user insights and data gathered if the experiment were configured correctly. Trust could erode for the engineering platform or A/B testing methodology if there's a history of bad tests resulting in invalid results. From a user perspective, a misconfigured test could introduce a broken user experience. The experimentation committee reviews each test to reduce these risks.

How does this compare to your reasons from the prior Analyst Task? From the For You A/B test experience, did you consider the potential for time wasted on data analysis if you later realize the test ended too early for the results to be statistically significant? If so, that's a great point!

You'll want the turnaround time of the committee's review to be quick. If it takes too long, teams are less likely to be incentivized to submit a test to the committee. You can mitigate this by having a checklist detailing the specifications for a committee member to review. Consider the checklist on page 137 for a step-by-step list of components to check to ensure a test is configured accurately.

Hypothesis: Does the test have a clear statement illustrating a specific, measurable goal?

 Eligibility Criteria: Is the criteria for the users to be allocated to the test and control variants defined?

 Metrics: Can a decision on whether to launch the change be accurately made with the success and guardrail metrics selected?

 Sample Size: Has the sample size been validated to ensure the results will be statistically valid?

 Duration: Is there a reasonable start and end date for the test? Is the test too short or too long?

 Team Contacts: If there's an issue with the test, who are the points of contact?

Let's say your experimentation review committee is ready to support A/B testing on your product, and you still need help to increase adoption. If this is the case, you may need to seek additional support elsewhere, such as executive sponsorship, which we'll explore in the next section.

Getting Executive Sponsorship

When advocating for an experimentation-driven culture, aim to get executive sponsorship from your leadership team. Find a leader who values curiosity and wants to support incorporating A/B testing as an integral part of the product development process. Once you have their support, leverage their communication channels for promoting the A/B testing platform. In practice, what this could include is the following:

- Present test results at company-wide meetings.

- Join product and engineering leadership meetings to highlight the value and benefits of A/B testing on the product.

- Create a pitch slide deck that includes user insights gained from A/B testing. Figure out what incentivizes teams and if A/B testing can support those incentives, then include those in the deck as well.

You can't shift a product engineering organization to embrace an experimentation-driven culture alone. The more support you get from leadership, the quicker adoption will be. Leadership sets the tone for an organization; if they are more open to taking risks and learning from failures, the general organization will align with their aspirations. So much of a team's behavior is based on incentives. If you want to change behavior, partner closely with a leader that can help create the right incentives to accelerate the adoption of A/B testing.

Identifying Companies That Already Embrace A/B Testing

If you're not A/B testing, your competitors are. Never underestimate the power of this statement. It can invoke a sense of urgency for your team to gain user and product insights as soon as possible.

Identify companies, whether they're your competitors or well-known companies, that are already using A/B testing to advocate for an experimentation culture. To start your market research, you could read company tech blogs to see if they've written about their experimentation platforms. Uber, Pinterest, StitchFix, and Etsy are examples of tech companies that have publicly available websites detailing their engineering efforts in the A/B testing domain. Alternatively, you could use the case studies from third-party A/B test products (typically documented on the third-party product's website).

Speaking of case studies, a paper titled "Online controlled experiments at large scale" describes a change made by a team that worked on the Bing search engine at Microsoft.[2] The change was small and took little effort to implement—the team increased the description length that accompanied an advertisement, providing more context for the user. It was a tiny change to the way advertisements were displayed on Bing that took little time to implement.

When the A/B test started, no one thought it would result in significant metrics gains. With these low expectations in mind, the test results were shocking! The data suggested a substantial increase in revenue—in the tens of millions! Bing's revenue increased by 12 percent. With this insight, the team became more informed and could deploy similar changes, hoping to have similar metric gains. If they hadn't evaluated such a small change, the cause for the metric increase would have been unclear. This is an excellent example of the benefit of evaluating any idea, whether small or big. Sometimes small changes have a significant effect on key metrics.

---

2.   https://dl.acm.org/doi/abs/10.1145/2487575.2488217

This narrative is also a great example of the value of making the process easy for executing A/B tests on a product. The easier the process is to run an A/B test, the less hesitancy your team will have to add this extra step to their product release cycle. When you understand the impact of changes, you'll have more confidence in future investments, as they'll be informed by past test results.

Knowing Your Audience

If you're in an organization resistant to adopting A/B testing, see what data is currently used to inform product decisions. Include those data points in the suite of available metrics in the A/B testing platform. Once people notice their metrics can be measured within your A/B testing platform, they're more likely to buy in.

For example, if the business team has a voice in how the product evolves, use the metrics they care about. If it's revenue, incorporate revenue in your data analysis. If it's measuring the diversity of content presented to the user, create a metric to enable these insights. These business-specific metrics don't need to be what you're optimizing for in your experiments, but they could be guardrail metrics to showcase that no harm has been done. Sometimes, uncertainty or fear of failure prevents us from making product changes. Data has the power to take that uncertainty and worry away.

During the CableMax For You A/B test, we grew a lot as an engineering team as we navigated through our first large-scale experiment. We got better at anticipating the concerns and questions our business and product stakeholders had with the test. For instance, as the business was concerned with revenue in the form of movies rented and purchased on the video product, we then started to incorporate total purchases and rentals as a guardrail metric. Including these additional metrics lessened concerns that the For You homepage would degrade purchase transactions on the product.

A research paper written by a team at LinkedIn titled "From Infrastructure to Culture: A/B Testing Challenges in Large Scale Social Networks" details the value of incorporating the same metrics that business teams care for within the experimentation platform. Specifically, take a look at the following statement from the paper:

By making our experiment results and business reports "comparable," we have made it possible for R&D teams to relate changes in business numbers with experiment launches. Moreover, the integration also provides the foundation that enables other organizations such as Finance to bake A/B test results into business forecasting.[3]

Suppose you notice that leaders at your job hesitate to use A/B testing. Perhaps they fear complicating the engineering stack or introducing too many if-else statements to enable features to be available to certain user groups. Or maybe they're more interested in monitoring engineering system performance than user engagement. If this is the case, you could research prior incidents to determine whether evaluating the issue that caused the incident could have been caught in an A/B test, similar to the CableMax production incident detailed in *Why You Should A/B Test*. To generalize a bit here, if your leaders care about engineering metrics, showcase that A/B testing can be used to evaluate engineering platforms. If your leaders care about business metrics, do the same, and create a narrative that highlights how business metrics can be included as a success or guardrail metric.

A/B testing can also be a method for reducing code that users rarely engage with. Let's say a feature is launched but has little engagement from a user's perspective. Wouldn't you rather know this early on by evaluating the change via an experiment versus letting the code stay in our ever-growing codebases? A feature which inherently equates to code that provides little value for our users should be removed from the product.

Another example is that your manager or peers are concerned about the decision-making process and how A/B testing could affect how product decisions are made. If this is the case, you could tell them that this will not replace decision-making but help inform product decisions. A/B testing doesn't replace the need for a strategy or product vision, but A/B testing does enable evaluating the tactics built for the product strategy to come to fruition. The results should inform how to steer your product vision so it becomes a reality.

Growing Demand for A/B Testing

For any engineering platform serving the needs of internal teams at a company to be successful, you need to treat the platform as a product. When you're marketing a new product, you'll take any opportunity to increase adoption.

To grow testing demand in your organization, you'll want to initially focus on your target audience. Who will be the first movers, the first people to opt in and evaluate their new idea with your A/B testing platform? That's step one;

---

3. https://content.linkedin.com/content/dam/engineering/site-assets/pdfs/ABTestingSocialNetwork_share.pdf

once you've identified your earlier adopters, you can have those same people be your ambassadors. They'll advocate and help with word of mouth. As your A/B testing platform continues to deliver test results, teams will return to run more tests.

Having a Driving Use Case for Your A/B Testing Platform

If you're in a platform organization in which your users are internal to the company, you have two types of adoption methods:

1. Early adopters who are pre-identified and have an initial use case driving the implementation.

2. Organic adoption that happens from word of mouth and results from other teams' successes.

At the early stages of employing A/B testing in an organization, it's best if you do not assume adoption. Everyone may not be excited to use your A/B testing platform. To combat this, you should pre-identify a team that can serve as the driving use case that will showcase the value of A/B testing as well as prevent the platform from not being used. Once you have a team that wants to run an A/B test, provide them with early access and ample support to ensure their experiment launches successfully. Having one successful A/B test will also bring credibility and trust to the platform, reducing fears or any other concerns that the engineering logic is faulty.

Look at your next task in the sidebar *Analyst Task: Brainstorm Reasons for Pre-identifying a Product Feature to A/B Test* for an example of what it looks like to have a driving use case that supports using A/B testing on a product.

Analyst Task: Brainstorm Reasons for Pre-identifying a Product Feature to A/B Test

In the case of the CableMax A/B testing platform, the personalization team's For You homepage was the driving use case. What do you think were the benefits of pre-identifying the For You homepage as the initial feature to motivate the implementation and design of the A/B testing platform? Brainstorm this before we detail it further in the following passage.

Having this important feature to evaluate its effectiveness on key product and business metrics motivated the team to ensure the A/B testing logic worked.

Having at least one team who is committed to using the platform will help with testing if the platform itself works. What other benefits of having a driving use case for the first A/B test did you identify? If you thought other teams would see the success of the For You A/B test and then mimic it with a similar A/B test, then you're right. That's what happened. The For You A/B test became the prime example for other teams to aspire to. After the personalization team's success, the sports team at CableMax ran an A/B test to evaluate their new feature. Then the business team started leveraging the platform to assess their targeting capabilities. The momentum continued to build and build until A/B testing became a first-class step in the product development life cycle.

Sharing User and Product Insights

You have to attract teams to use the A/B testing platform to grow demand. A low-effort tactic to increase curiosity is to overshare A/B test results. You can send out a newsletter in the form of a monthly email to the product and engineering organization that highlights past experiments. Make sure to include successful experiments that led to launching the new feature and experiments that negatively impacted key metrics and did not result in a product launch. Writing a monthly newsletter will spread the word and lower the barrier to accessing the key user and product insights gained from running A/B tests on the product.

Being the Catalyst for Change

Keep in mind that your first A/B test use case will more than likely be the hardest to advocate for. At CableMax, no one trusted the results produced by the A/B testing platform. This translated to no one trusting the effect the For You homepage had on product and business metrics.

If you're in an organization similar to the one described in the CableMax example, it will take a while to make this change happen. The For You homepage took a year to launch to all users of the video product. This extended timeline wasn't a result of the technology or process but rather the lack of trust in the data and A/B testing process because experimentation wasn't a critical step in the product development life cycle. Features were built and then shipped straight to production for all users to engage with. Would it have been quicker to ship the For You homepage straight to production without A/B testing? Yes. Would the same user insights gained from the A/B test, including the key learning demonstrating that the For You homepage is better suited for active users on the product, have been discovered? No, definitely not.

It's not easy to shift the mindset of those used to operating without A/B testing. You can use the tactics shared throughout this chapter to ease this change. The more thought you put into your engineering platform so that it's easy to run experiments, the less costly it will be for teams to set up those experiments and the more likely they'll decide to introduce this step into their product development life cycle. The technology you build to enable A/B testing directly influences the process. The easier the process, the more likely people will opt in. See the following figure on how humans, technology, and process are the three major factors in cultivating test-friendly culture.

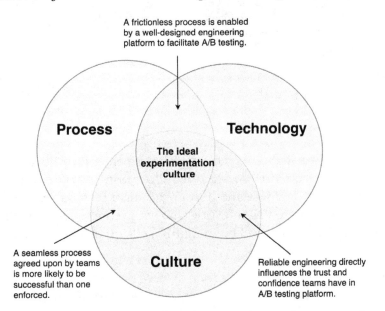

Let's consider areas you may need to focus on to create an experimentation culture at your job in the sidebar *Chapter Roundup: What Obstacles Are You Anticipating When Introducing A/B Testing?*

Chapter Roundup: What Obstacles Are You Anticipating When Introducing A/B Testing?

Considering the three key areas reflected in the figure on page 143, what area do you think you need to lean into most to enable an experimentation-driven culture at your job? While considering this question, consider the following:

- Is the reliability of the engineering platform to properly facilitate A/B tests on the product top of mind for your teammates and peers? If so, you should prioritize technology when integrating A/B testing into your product development life cycle.

- Is there trust in the data and test results produced from the A/B testing platform? If not, then add an extra step to the experimentation committee to review if the metrics and configuration of the test are valid. While doing this, it's also worth considering incorporating a step in the A/B testing process that encourages teams to share their data analysis. The more people know, the more comfortable they'll be with the process and results.

- Is your team used to the executives deciding what gets built and shipped to production? If that's the case, find a leader who believes in A/B testing and have them advocate for engineers, product owners, designers, and anyone at the company to pitch ideas for teams to evaluate via a minimal prototype in an A/B testing context.

Adapting how your team releases changes to your users isn't easy, but it's well worth it once you start reaping all the benefits of A/B testing.

Wrapping Up

Here we are—it's the end of the chapter and the end of the book! The days of pushing changes to production without an A/B test, unaware of how changes influence important business and user engagement metrics, will be long gone. Once you've incorporated A/B testing into your team's way of working, both your team and your users will be thankful. Let's quickly review what we covered in this chapter:

- How to create an experimentation review committee and the benefits of employing such to roll out A/B testing at your company.

- How to combat concerns about the time spent on A/B testing by building prototypes for quicker iterations and insights.

- How to make the A/B testing process more accessible with a standardized template that lowers the barrier of entry so that anyone can run an A/B test.

In this book, you've discovered many practical concepts needed to facilitate A/B testing on a product. You explored the anatomy of an A/B test and the basic software components required to orchestrate the experimentation process on a product. You uncovered the benefits of A/B testing and different tests to measure different outcomes. You've also done a great job navigating the analyst tasks within each chapter.

The last step is to continue with your A/B testing journey! With each test, you will notice an increase in complexity as you progress in using this experimentation methodology to evaluate product changes. From statistical distribution to causal inference, there's a lot more to learn when observing your test outcomes. As you continue these practices, you'll transition from an A/B testing novice to a confident practitioner. You'll find it hard to believe you once put changes into production without measuring the effect on your users, product, and business.

Happy A/B testing!

Thank you!

We hope you enjoyed this book and that you're already thinking about what you want to learn next. To help make that decision easier, we're offering you this gift.

Head on over to https://pragprog.com right now, and use the coupon code BUYANOTHER2023 to save 30% on your next ebook. Offer is void where prohibited or restricted. This offer does not apply to any edition of the *The Pragmatic Programmer* ebook.

And if you'd like to share your own expertise with the world, why not propose a writing idea to us? After all, many of our best authors started off as our readers, just like you. With up to a 50% royalty, world-class editorial services, and a name you trust, there's nothing to lose. Visit https://pragprog.com/become-an-author/ today to learn more and to get started.

We thank you for your continued support, and we hope to hear from you again soon!

The Pragmatic Bookshelf

SAVE 30%!
Use coupon code
BUYANOTHER2023

Programming Machine Learning

You've decided to tackle machine learning — because you're job hunting, embarking on a new project, or just think self-driving cars are cool. But where to start? It's easy to be intimidated, even as a software developer. The good news is that it doesn't have to be that hard. Conquer machine learning by writing code one line at a time, from simple learning programs all the way to a true deep learning system. Tackle the hard topics by breaking them down so they're easier to understand, and build your confidence by getting your hands dirty.

Paolo Perrotta
(340 pages) ISBN: 9781680506600. $47.95
https://pragprog.com/book/pplearn

Design It!

Don't engineer by coincidence—design it like you mean it! Grounded by fundamentals and filled with practical design methods, this is the perfect introduction to software architecture for programmers who are ready to grow their design skills. Ask the right stakeholders the right questions, explore design options, share your design decisions, and facilitate collaborative workshops that are fast, effective, and fun. Become a better programmer, leader, and designer. Use your new skills to lead your team in implementing software with the right capabilities—and develop awesome software!

Michael Keeling
(358 pages) ISBN: 9781680502091. $41.95
https://pragprog.com/book/mkdsa

Designed for Use, Second Edition

This book is for designers, developers, and product
managers who are charged with what sometimes seems
like an impossible task: making sure products work
the way your users expect them to. You'll find out how
to design applications and websites that people will
not only use, but will absolutely love. The second edition brings the book up to date and expands it with
three completely new chapters.

Lukas Mathis
(338 pages) ISBN: 9781680501605. $38
https://pragprog.com/book/lmuse2

Your Code as a Crime Scene

Jack the Ripper and legacy codebases have more in
common than you'd think. Inspired by forensic psychology methods, this book teaches you strategies to predict the future of your codebase, assess refactoring
direction, and understand how your team influences
the design. With its unique blend of forensic psychology
and code analysis, this book arms you with the
strategies you need, no matter what programming
language you use.

Adam Tornhill
(218 pages) ISBN: 9781680500387. $36
https://pragprog.com/book/atcrime

Creating Software with Modern Diagramming Techniques

Diagrams communicate relationships more directly and clearly than words ever can. Using only text-based markup, create meaningful and attractive diagrams to document your domain, visualize user flows, reveal system architecture at any desired level, or refactor your code. With the tools and techniques this book will give you, you'll create a wide variety of diagrams in minutes, share them with others, and revise and update them immediately on the basis of feedback. Adding diagrams to your professional vocabulary will enable you to work through your ideas quickly when working on your own code or discussing a proposal with colleagues.

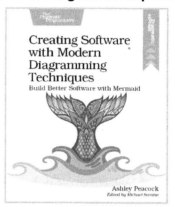

Ashley Peacock
(156 pages) ISBN: 9781680509830. $29.95
https://pragprog.com/book/apdiag

Domain Modeling Made Functional

You want increased customer satisfaction, faster development cycles, and less wasted work. Domain-driven design (DDD) combined with functional programming is the innovative combo that will get you there. In this pragmatic, down-to-earth guide, you'll see how applying the core principles of functional programming can result in software designs that model real-world requirements both elegantly and concisely—often more so than an object-oriented approach. Practical examples in the open-source F# functional language, and examples from familiar business domains, show you how to apply these techniques to build software that is business-focused, flexible, and high quality.

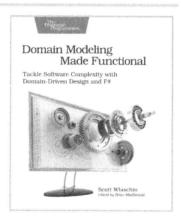

Scott Wlaschin
(310 pages) ISBN: 9781680502541. $47.95
https://pragprog.com/book/swdddf

Designing Data Governance from the Ground Up

Businesses own more data than ever before, but it's of no value if you don't know how to use it. Data governance manages the people, processes, and strategy needed for deploying data projects to production. But doing it well is far from easy: Less than one fourth of business leaders say their organizations are data driven. In *Designing Data Governance from the Ground Up*, you'll build a cross-functional strategy to create roadmaps and stewardship for data-focused projects, embed data governance into your engineering practice, and put processes in place to monitor data after deployment.

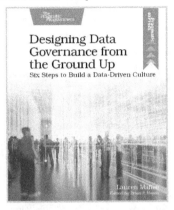

Lauren Maffeo
(100 pages) ISBN: 9781680509809. $29.95
https://pragprog.com/book/lmmlops

Concurrent Data Processing in Elixir

Learn different ways of writing concurrent code in Elixir and increase your application's performance, without sacrificing scalability or fault-tolerance. Most projects benefit from running background tasks and processing data concurrently, but the world of OTP and various libraries can be challenging. Which Supervisor and what strategy to use? What about GenServer? Maybe you need back-pressure, but is GenStage, Flow, or Broadway a better choice? You will learn everything you need to know to answer these questions, start building highly concurrent applications in no time, and write code that's not only fast, but also resilient to errors and easy to scale.

Svilen Gospodinov
(174 pages) ISBN: 9781680508192. $39.95
https://pragprog.com/book/sgdpelixir

Designing Elixir Systems with OTP

You know how to code in Elixir; now learn to think in
it. Learn to design libraries with intelligent layers that
shape the right data structures, flow from one function
into the next, and present the right APIs. Embrace the
same OTP that's kept our telephone systems reliable
and fast for over 30 years. Move beyond understanding
the OTP functions to knowing what's happening under
the hood, and why that matters. Using that knowledge,
instinctively know how to design systems that deliver
fast and resilient services to your users, all with an
Elixir focus.

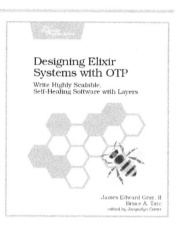

James Edward Gray, II and Bruce A. Tate
(246 pages) ISBN: 9781680506617. $41.95
https://pragprog.com/book/jgotp

Functional Web Development with Elixir, OTP, and Phoenix

Elixir and Phoenix are generating tremendous excitement as an unbeatable platform for building modern
web applications. For decades OTP has helped developers create incredibly robust, scalable applications with
unparalleled uptime. Make the most of them as you
build a stateful web app with Elixir, OTP, and Phoenix.
Model domain entities without an ORM or a database.
Manage server state and keep your code clean with
OTP Behaviours. Layer on a Phoenix web interface
without coupling it to the business logic. Open doors
to powerful new techniques that will get you thinking
about web development in fundamentally new ways.

Lance Halvorsen
(218 pages) ISBN: 9781680502435. $45.95
https://pragprog.com/book/lhelph

Modern CSS with Tailwind, Second Edition

Tailwind CSS is an exciting new CSS framework that allows you to design your site by composing simple utility classes to create complex effects. With Tailwind, you can style your text, move your items on the page, design complex page layouts, and adapt your design for devices from a phone to a wide-screen monitor. With this book, you'll learn how to use the Tailwind for its flexibility and its consistency, from the smallest detail of your typography to the entire design of your site.

Noel Rappin
(102 pages) ISBN: 9781680509403. $29.95
https://pragprog.com/book/tailwind2

Pythonic Programming

Make your good Python code even better by following proven and effective pythonic programming tips. Avoid logical errors that usually go undetected by Python linters and code formatters, such as frequent data look-ups in long lists, improper use of local and global variables, and mishandled user input. Discover rare language features, like rational numbers, set comprehensions, counters, and pickling, that may boost your productivity. Discover how to apply general programming patterns, including caching, in your Python code. Become a better-than-average Python programmer, and develop self-documented, maintainable, easy-to-understand programs that are fast to run and hard to break.

Dmitry Zinoviev
(150 pages) ISBN: 9781680508611. $26.95
https://pragprog.com/book/dzpythonic

The Pragmatic Bookshelf

The Pragmatic Bookshelf features books written by professional developers for professional developers. The titles continue the well-known Pragmatic Programmer style and continue to garner awards and rave reviews. As development gets more and more difficult, the Pragmatic Programmers will be there with more titles and products to help you stay on top of your game.

Visit Us Online

This Book's Home Page
https://pragprog.com/book/abtest
Source code from this book, errata, and other resources. Come give us feedback, too!

Keep Up-to-Date
https://pragprog.com
Join our announcement mailing list (low volume) or follow us on Twitter @pragprog for new titles, sales, coupons, hot tips, and more.

New and Noteworthy
https://pragprog.com/news
Check out the latest Pragmatic developments, new titles, and other offerings.

Save on the ebook

Save on the ebook versions of this title. Owning the paper version of this book entitles you to purchase the electronic versions at a terrific discount.

PDFs are great for carrying around on your laptop—they are hyperlinked, have color, and are fully searchable. Most titles are also available for the iPhone and iPod touch, Amazon Kindle, and other popular e-book readers.

Send a copy of your receipt to support@pragprog.com and we'll provide you with a discount coupon.

Contact Us

Online Orders:	*https://pragprog.com/catalog*
Customer Service:	*support@pragprog.com*
International Rights:	*translations@pragprog.com*
Academic Use:	*academic@pragprog.com*
Write for Us:	*http://write-for-us.pragprog.com*
Or Call:	+1 800-699-7764

Printed in the USA
CPSIA information can be obtained
at www.ICGtesting.com
JSHW052339110923
48262JS00007BA/43

9 798888 650080